MW01061772

ten poems
for
difficult times

ten poems
for
difficult times

ROGER HOUSDEN

New World Library
Novato, California

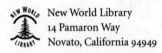 New World Library
14 Pamaron Way
Novato, California 94949

Text design by Tona Pearce-Myers

Library of Congress Cataloging-in-Publication Data is available.

First printing, March 2018
ISBN 978-1-60868-529-5
Ebook ISBN 978-1-60868-530-1
Printed in Canada on 100% postconsumer-waste recycled paper

 New World Library is proud to be a Gold Certified Environmentally Responsible Publisher. Publisher certification awarded by Green Press Initiative. www.greenpressinitiative.org

10   9   8   7   6   5   4   3   2   1

CONTENTS

Why Poetry for Difficult Times?

Poetry is a concise and elemental means of expressing the deepest of human emotions: joy, sorrow, grief, hope, love, and longing. It connects us as a people and a community; it speaks for us in a way few other forms of writing can do. When I was in the process of moving to Manhattan in 2001, in the weeks after 9/11, poems appeared on every available wall in the city. Yet even though I was so aware of poetry's power, over the next ten years, while sitting alone in front of my computer, finishing up another volume in my Ten Poems series, I would wonder at times whether I was wasting my time.

After all, the world is in trouble. It has always been in trouble. Not only that, but we are often in trouble personally, too. Surely there must be something more useful, more pressing, to give my time to than reflecting on poetry? Couldn't I go start a project in Africa, or at least do some small thing to prevent climate catastrophe, start reducing my own carbon footprint, for example, and begin a movement to encourage others to do the same? But no; I wrote more poetry books, wondering all the while whether they and I were doing little more than making ourselves progressively irrelevant.

I knew better, which is why I kept writing. I knew that great poetry has the power to start a fire in a person's life. It can alter the way we see ourselves. It can change the way we see the world. You may never have read a poem in your life, and yet you can pick up a volume, open it to any page, and suddenly find yourself blown into a world full of awe, dread, wonder, marvel, deep sorrow, and joy. Poetry not only matters; it is profoundly necessary. *Especially* in times of darkness and difficulty, both personal and collective. To read or write poetry is a powerful, even subversive, act, and it is one small thing we can do that can make a very big difference.

It can make a difference because at its best poetry calls forth our deep Being, bids us to live by its promptings. It dares us to break free from the safe strategies of the cautious mind, from our default attitudes and beliefs. It calls to us, like the wild geese, as Mary Oliver would say, from an open sky. It is a magical art, and always has been — a making of language spells designed to open our eyes, open our doors, and welcome us into a bigger world, one of possibilities we may never have dreamed of. This is also why poetry can be dangerous: we may never be the same again after reading a poem that speaks to our own life directly. I know that when I meet my own life in a great poem, I feel opened, clarified, confirmed, somehow, in what I always sensed was true but had no words for. Anything that can do this is surely necessary for the fullness of a human life.

The word *poet* means a "maker" — someone who crafts language into a shape. The word *maker* has the same etymological root as the words *matrix*, and *magic*, and it's true that the sound, the rhythm, of good poetry is literally spellbinding. It lulls, it sways, it rises and falls, and our hearts and minds rise and fall along with it. Poetry literally entrains us into the energy, the mood, the vibration, even, that the poet conjures with her words and images. The subtler and more refined that energy is, the more it can raise us to the best that we are. That it does so is another reason poetry is so necessary today, when we need our best selves more than ever.

Poetry revitalizes our imagination. A hundred years ago, when Yeats was alive, the imagination was far more of a common currency than it is today. The imagination today is under siege. Our political leaders, steeped in doublespeak and alternative facts, have brought George Orwell's *1984* closer than ever. We are saturated with both false and genuine information and find it a challenge to tell the difference. We are saturated with concepts and opinions that stream ready-formed from Facebook or Twitter, which siphon our attention into an abstract metaworld divorced from concrete reality. People engage less and less with the natural environment, less and less with each other in community, relying more and more for their experience on the received knowledge that comes on a screen or down a wire.

No wonder the imagination is in danger of shriveling to the size of a pea. Imagination feeds on the smell of old tree roots, on conversation, on barking dogs, on the cries of children. Poetry's fuel is the imagination; it uses the things of this concrete world for its material and then reaches down into the layers of meaning that any object or person contains. Pablo Neruda wrote an ode to a lemon, to his socks, to laziness, to a tomato, to salt, and more. Poetry shows us that not just the gods but the humblest forms in the world can reveal enough truth and beauty to fill us with praise and awe.

Poetry rescues the world from oblivion by the practice of attention. Our attention honors and gives value to living things, gives them their proper name and particularity, retrieves them from the obscurity of the general. When I pay attention, something in me awakens, and that something is much closer to who I am than the driven or drifting self I usually take myself to be. When I pay attention, I am straightened, somehow, brought into a deeper life.

Poetry takes a stand against the increasing homogenization of world cultures because it is the speech of one specific individual in his unique voice. The sweeping homogenization and commodification of everything may be one reason that there are more poetry festivals, slams, groups, readings, and creative writing courses than ever before. Poetry is the expression of one person's irreplaceable subjective sensibility, another name for which is *soul*. It is the creation of one sensibility, giving form to how it feels to be oneself and to see the world through one's own eyes in the most precise language one can summon.

Everyday language usually fails to do this well. But poetry reaches with its sounds and rhythms down below the realm of the conscious mind to awaken and nourish the imagination. Poetry is imagination's language, and as such, it is prophetic speech. In essence, what is found there is our deep humanity, which binds us in empathy for others, however different they may appear to be from us. In everyday language, we might say to someone, for example, "I feel sick," which doesn't tell the listener very much and doesn't allow her to feel very much. But the poet Robert Lowell says it this way:

> *I hear my ill spirit sob in each blood cell*

Poetry says the unsayable. Lowell makes clear the nature of his sickness; it is a sickness of soul, one that pervades the body. And as the poet Mark Doty observes in the essay "Why Poetry Matters Now," Lowell's sickness sobs, and the sobbing is accentuated by the twelve vowels in that sentence, the alliteration of the *b*s and the *l*s. All this makes the line thick and heavy in the mouth, Doty says, which is what sobbing does. Try saying it, and see what a mouthful it is. Lowell gives us the visceral experience, not just the information that he is sick.

Lowell's line comes from the idiosyncratic stuff of his selfhood — from the unique soul of Lowell. Someone else would speak to sickness in a different way. Here is Sylvia Plath on having a fever:

> *I am a lantern —*
> *My head a moon*
> *Of Japanese paper. My gold beaten skin*
> *Infinitely delicate and infinitely expensive.*[1]

The metaphors come tumbling over one other. She steps out of her body, it seems, and makes of it something other — a lantern, which then becomes something other — a moon.

This is a long way from Lowell, but it's another world altogether from the blunt vagueness of "I feel sick." The difference between the two poets is one of voice. And by the writer's voice we mean the way the particular texture of subjective perception finds its way into speech.

Who knows how the image of a lantern came to Plath. She likely didn't know. Poems are a window into the soul because they honor the unknown, both in us and in the world. They come from the deep waters below the surface; they are shaped into form by the power of language and set free to fly with wings of images and metaphor. Imagine a world in which everything was already known. It would be a dead world, no questions, no wonder, no other possibilities. That's what my own world can feel like sometimes when my imagination has gone into retreat. I, like you, no doubt, have discovered that poetry is a phoenix I can fly on to return to that forgotten land.

Poetry uses words that are known to all of us but in a sequence and order that surprises us out of our normal speech rhythms and linear thought processes. Poetry uniquely combines imaginative power and conscious intelligence, inspiration and hard work, and its effect is to illuminate our lives and breathe new life, new seeing, new tasting into the world we thought we knew. Poetry bids us to eat the apple whole.

Poems like the ones in this book shake me awake. They

pass on their attentiveness, their insight, their love of this broken world to me, the reader. We can wake up to the world and to ourselves in a new way by reading poems such as these — especially when we read them aloud, and shape the sounds on our lips and the rhythms on our breath — making us more fully human. The poet Jane Hirshfield says, "Whether from reading the New England Transcendentalists or Eskimo poetry, I feel that everything I know about being human has been deepened by the poems I've read."[2]

John Keats speaks of this humanizing power, too, when he says, "Poetry should strike the reader as a wording of his own highest thoughts, and appear almost as a Remembrance."[3]

That's all very well, you might say. Poems may be a humanizing influence, they may even carry us to the heights of spiritual insight and realization, but what have they done to shift the world's obsession with power, greed, and violence? What has a poem done to dissolve injustice? This argument has been rising and falling for centuries, but it is worth our notice that poetry and literature in general have been routinely banned around the world at various times because of their subversive influence. If poetry and literature are humanizing influences, they work directly against those regimes and ideologies that restrict rather than encourage liberty and justice. Nazim Hikmet, whose poem "It's This Way" is in this book, spent eighteen years in a Turkish prison for his beliefs. Because poetry connects different worlds, different ideas, and different people and things, it generates empathy — empathy with others and with all living things. When, through a poetic act of imagination, one feels kinship with others and with all life, it is that much more difficult to oppress others; and that, in a tyrannical regime, is subversion.

Stalin tried to strip Russia of its soul with his death camps. Poet Osip Mandelstam restored that soul by reciting poetry to his fellow convicts and by writing about it in his journal. "Perhaps to remain a poet in such circumstances," Saul Bellow writes, "is also to reach the heart of politics. The human feelings, human experiences, the human form and face, recover their proper place — the foreground."[4]

That, after all, is what politics is ultimately about — human feelings and the human form. Poetry can give a human face to our collective struggles and remind us that this human world is not only broken, it is beautiful. That is what the poems in this volume do. There's a headstone in a Long Island graveyard — the one where Jackson Pollock is buried — that I think encapsulates the value and necessity of poetry in a world of sorrows: "Artists and poets are the raw nerve ends of humanity. By themselves they can do little to save humanity. Without them there would be little worth saving."

1.

GOOD BONES

by Maggie Smith

Life is short, though I keep this from my children.
Life is short, and I've shortened mine
in a thousand delicious, ill-advised ways,
a thousand deliciously ill-advised ways
I'll keep from my children. The world is at least
fifty percent terrible, and that's a conservative
estimate, though I keep this from my children.
For every bird there is a stone thrown at a bird.
For every loved child, a child broken, bagged,
sunk in a lake. Life is short and the world
is at least half terrible, and for every kind
stranger, there is one who would break you,
though I keep this from my children. I am trying
to sell them the world. Any decent realtor,
walking you through a real shithole, chirps on
about good bones: This place could be beautiful,
right? You could make this place beautiful.

DON'T TELL THE CHILDREN

It is surely a writer's dream: to publish a work that by sheer coincidence or synchronicity strikes the mother lode of public attention by giving voice to an emerging mood in the zeitgeist. Perhaps an unexpected event, either tragic or celebratory, galvanizes a nation. Perhaps the moon shines green for a night, everyone out in the streets looking up at the sky, mouths open wide, and it just so happens that a line straight out of your new poem speaks to such a moon.

A writer, no more than anyone else, never knows which way the wind will blow, never knows if her work is destined to disappear forever into the netherworld of the great unread, or whether it happens by some curious concatenation of events to have found, unwittingly, the precise words and mood to foreshadow a collective joy or tragedy, and thereby be destined to leap from pages everywhere, to general public acclaim. At the time of writing, however, these concerns barely exist, if at all. All that matters then is the music of the next line.

In summer 2015, Maggie Smith, a freelance writer and editor with an MFA from Ohio State, was sitting in a Starbucks in her hometown of Bexley, Ohio, not far from Columbus. She wrote the first line of a new poem — "Life is short, though I keep this from my children." The rest of the poem flowed easily from there, so that by the time she left the coffee shop she had a new piece of work that had come out whole.

A year later, in June 2016, as a gunman killed forty-nine people at the Pulse nightclub in Orlando and British politician Jo Cox was murdered in broad daylight at a constituency meeting in the north of England, Smith's poem "Good Bones" was published in the online journal *Waxwing*.

A reader touched by the poem's message posted a screenshot on Facebook, where a Brooklyn-based musician read it and passed it along on Twitter. Articles about the poem quickly appeared in *The Guardian*, *Slate*, and elsewhere, helping to spread the poem worldwide.

Since then the poem has been interpreted by a dance troupe in India, turned into a musical score for the voice and harp, and translated into Spanish, Italian, French, Korean, Hindi, Tamil, Telugu, and Malayalam. Smith, whose poetry was known only by poetry aficionados before the publication of "Good Bones," suddenly found herself an international celebrity. In the months after the poem's publication she was invited to speak at book festivals and conferences around the country and in Europe. Public Radio International called "Good Bones" "the official poem of 2016." Then along came the shock of the 2016 election, and her poem took off into the blogosphere again, rippling out onto the radio and into media everywhere.

In November 2016 it became one of the three most down-loaded poems on the site of the American Academy of Poets. "Good Bones" has become something of a societal anxiety barometer. "I can tell something bad is happening in the world when my poem is surging," Smith, a thirty-nine-year-old mother of two, told Nora Krug of *The Washington Post.*

On the day after the 2016 election, *Vox* published a post headlined "Feeling terrible right now? Maybe some poetry will help." *The Guardian* had one listing "poems to counter the election fallout — and beyond." The *Huffington Post*, for its part, offered "18 Compassionate Poems to Help You Weather Uncertain Times."

Poetry often bubbles up at germinal moments in an individual's life, too, even if that person has never read or written poetry before. When Kobe Bryant retired, the first thing he did was to write a love poem to basketball. Poetry allows us to express the inexpressible, to bring into essential form thoughts and feelings that have swarmed our mind.

Yet Smith hadn't been thinking about world events at all while writing those lines in Starbucks. She was thinking about her family. "It was a poem written from the perspective of one mother feeling anxious about how to raise kids, and explain a world to them that is as wonderful as it is terrible," she told *The Washington Post.* "How to keep the worst parts from them while they're young while not lying to them."

Her four-year-old can't read yet, so he doesn't know what the fuss is about. Her daughter, though, is eight, and she has read the poem. They've discussed it, a little. "She was really disappointed in the outcome of the election, and we have talked a little bit about when things don't go our way how we can work small to make big change," says Smith. "Just doing your best at school, and being kind to others, if we all do those small things, it will make a difference. So that's sort of my explaining it to an eight-year-old version of things.

"I've been writing out of the experience of watching my children read the world like a book they've just opened. They are seeing everything for the first time, and through them I am seeing with fresh eyes. They ask pointed questions, like: What is the earth for?"

Smith wrote "Good Bones" with fresh eyes, which explains why it has caught the public imagination and why it is so indelible. The sentiments themselves are hardly original and may not seem especially profound: *This is a savage and yet beautiful world.* We have only to look around us to know that this is true. Or to watch the Oscar-winning short documentary *White Helmets* and see Russian pilots with all the time in the world lazily dropping cluster bombs on men in white helmets who have dedicated their lives to rescuing those beneath the rubble of Aleppo. The men in the sky and the men on the ground are in the same movie at the same time.

We know this, except we forget. We do not stop to look around us. Maggie Smith has said that one of her favorite lines is in Ada Limón's poem "The Same Thing": "You say you love the world, so love the world." The way Smith loves the world, she says, is by paying attention, and by finding ways

— formally, rhetorically, lyrically — to write about her own experience, on her own terms. She follows, that is to say, in the footsteps of the great Mary Oliver, who in her poem "The Summer Day" writes:

> *I don't know exactly what a prayer is.*
> *I do know how to pay attention.*

The point of "Good Bones" — and of other poems in this book that address a similar theme, such as Jack Gilbert's "A Brief for the Defense" and Wendell Berry's "Now You Know the Worst"— is not to give us information but a visceral experience of an existential and timeless truth. In his poem "Of Asphodel, That Greeny Flower," William Carlos Williams writes:

> *My heart rouses*
> > *thinking to bring you news*
> > > *of something*
> *that concerns you*
> > *and concerns many men. Look at*
> > > *what passes for the new.*
> *You will not find it there but in*
> > *despised poems.*
> > > *It is difficult*
> *to get the news from poems*
> > *yet men die miserably every day*
> > > *for lack*
> *of what is found there.*

"Good Bones" is not meant for the mind alone; it is meant to score a direct hit on the great heart of compassion found in all of us, the broken-open heart willing to pay attention to the unspeakable sorrows of this world, to look on the horrors we visit upon each other and yet to praise this human life anyway. Because this life is all we have.

Or would you rather be a fish and be done with the bother of empathy? Smith makes her choice in this poem, in plain terms. She does it with humor, in terse phrases, and with frequent repetition — not just as a rhythmic device but to drum it into our bones so we do not forget: Life is short. We don't have time for protracted discussions on the matter or for avoiding what is right before our eyes. Life asks us to open our arms to both the beauty and the beast and to respond in whichever ways our life makes available to us. If you are the captain of a boat on a Greek island, maybe you can rescue refugees from the Mediterranean. If you are a poet, maybe you can write poems. If you are an eight-year-old or an eighty-year-old, maybe you can practice being kind.

One of the reasons "Good Bones" has had such traction is that it directly addresses our responsibility toward our children, the future generations. How do we prepare them for the dramas they will encounter both in their own lives and in the world? "How to keep the worst parts from them while they're young, while not lying to them," as Maggie Smith said in the *Washington Post* interview. Every parent is faced with this dilemma, especially now that children are exposed daily to tragedies and injustices around the world.

Jason Gardner, my editor, told me about his ten-year-old son, who anxiously asked him about climate change. "He's heard enough about it that he finally asked if I thought all the ice at the North and South Poles would eventually melt. I said I didn't know, but that it is melting, and lots of people are trying to do something about it. I tried to be hopeful, even though I don't really feel hopeful myself. Because pessimism doesn't do anything, and I certainly want to instill a fighting spirit in my children. Honestly, though, I don't think anything I said made him feel any better. That was painful to realize."

Maggie Smith uses a wry, matter-of-fact humor to keep our keel even in the stormy sea of her subject.

> *Life is short, and I've shortened mine*
> *in a thousand delicious, ill-advised ways,*
> *a thousand deliciously ill-advised ways*
> *I'll keep from my children. The world is at least*
> *fifty percent terrible, and that's a conservative*
> *estimate, though I keep this from my children.*

Having prepared us with generalities, she ventures into deeper waters. She acknowledges without flinching the awful reality of specific truths:

> *For every bird there is a stone thrown at a bird.*
> *For every loved child, a child broken, bagged,*
> *sunk in a lake. [...]*

for every kind
stranger, there is one who would break you.

And why does she keep this from her children? Because she wants them to know and believe what she herself knows and believes: that this world is worth living for, in spite of everything.

Her final metaphor is a stroke of pure poetic inspiration that drives the point home in the most deceptively prosaic way. This earth is prime real estate. It's got good bones. With a little imagination, it's got all the makings of your own little slice of paradise. Yes, it's a fixer-upper, it's true. It needs a paint job and, yes, some significant remodeling here and there. It's an old house, and there will always be repairs to do. But it's got good bones. The foundations are sound. It could be beautiful. In the final line Smith speaks to her children and turns the work over to the next generation:

You could make this place beautiful.

2.

THE THING IS

by Ellen Bass

to love life, to love it even
when you have no stomach for it
and everything you've held dear
crumbles like burnt paper in your hands,
your throat filled with the silt of it.
When grief sits with you, its tropical heat
thickening the air, heavy as water
more fit for gills than lungs;
when grief weights you like your own flesh
only more of it, an obesity of grief,
you think, How can a body withstand this?
Then you hold life like a face
between your palms, a plain face,
no charming smile, no violet eyes,
and you say, yes, I will take you
I will love you, again.

REMEMBER THIS

Whether she has ever sat on her haunches for an hour or so, Ellen Bass uses poetry in the way of a Zen practitioner. She uses it to engage with her life experience as sharply and as clearly as the moment allows. And as simply, too. Like Bashō, in this haiku, for example:

> *An old silent pond...*
> *A frog jumps into the pond,*
> *splash! Silence again.*
> (Translated by Harry Behn)

Or like William Carlos Williams, a doctor but no Buddhist, in his poem about

> *a red wheel*
> *barrow*
>
> *glazed with rain*
> *water*

To take another example from Ellen Bass's body of work, her poem "Gate C22" begins like this:

> *At gate C22 in the Portland airport*
> *a man in a broad-band leather hat kissed*
> *a woman arriving from Orange County.*

As we keep reading it becomes clear that the difference between the gaze of Ellen Bass and that of a Bashō or a Williams is that her eyes look inward as well as outward. Bashō's *splash* leaves a wordless ripple in my mind; William's *wheelbarrow* lodges itself in my visual cortex and prompts me to see the world as shorn of associations as he does. Just a wheelbarrow, marvelous in its wheelbarrow-ness, signifying nothing, and yet not less than everything. With the couple in "Gate C22," kissing away in Portland airport, Bass does something different. The couple set off a chain of felt responses inside her, which she then brought to us in a series of vivid images that yoke both the outer scene and the inner experience of it.

It's the same with her poem "The Thing Is." Bass takes us down into her interior landscape, leading us step-by-step, one image and metaphor at a time, as clearly and unequivocally as a Bashō haiku does in the outer world. Perhaps her mother died, or she lost a lover or a dear friend. Perhaps she just heard the news about 9/11. Whatever it was, something must have happened for her to write this poem, because it has the weight — the authenticity — of personal suffering and experience running through it like a red seam.

Yet I don't even need to know the details, because Bass has used whatever personal tragedy may have darkened her days to swim down to the bottom of the well of grief and come up with the bright coins of images that speak a universal language, recognizable to anyone who has suffered loss — which is all of us.

That first image — which I can taste as well as feel in my clenched hand and in my throat —

> *everything you've held dear*
> *crumbles like burnt paper in your hands,*
> *your throat filled with the silt of it.*

reminds me of these lines in the poem "Kindness" by Naomi Shihab Nye:

> *Before you know what kindness really is*
> *you must lose things,*
> *feel the future dissolve in a moment*
> *like salt in a weakened broth.*

Bass's crumbling burnt paper, Nye's future dissolving "like salt in a weakened broth," point me to the stark truth that everything, everything I hold in my hand will fall away, as I, too, will fall away, and all too soon. Bass uses just four vivid words to pierce me through with this truth we would all much rather avoid. "Crumbles like burnt paper" — the image burns itself not just into my mind but into my gut. This is not philosophy we are talking here, not some platitude about everything passing. This is a visceral reality that, as Bass says, we "have no stomach for." I love this quality of Ellen Bass's work. It is always rooted in the body and in the senses. And yet it relies on attentiveness, on presence of mind, to be conscious of what she experiences in her body and all around her.

That's why I think of her as a Zen poet. What other response to the dissolving world would a Zen poet have than to love it, in spite of everything? That's the thing, isn't it? To love what we have because it is all we have: this gain, that loss, this love, these tears, this joy, even when we have no stomach for it. Especially then.

We lose people and partners and jobs and beliefs and hair and organs and vitality and hope for the world and the vision of what our country could be but is not; and we grieve, and rightly so, necessarily so, even though — especially though — we know we will lose everything anyway. Jack Gilbert says this in his poem "The Lost Hotels of Paris":

The Lord gives everything and charges
by taking it back. What a bargain.

Well, yes, if you put it that way, life itself is on loan, free and without interest; except in difficult times it doesn't always feel like much of a bargain. Seeing it Gilbert's way requires a rare wisdom. It normally takes a while before we can see the gift in adversity, if indeed we ever do. In the end the only gift that really delivers on its promise is the one Ellen Bass's poem praises here, which is loving life down to its dregs, no matter what. Because in the end we have nothing to lose by doing so.

That doesn't mean that we can just skip over our sorrow. Bass brings us to the necessity of falling to our knees under the weight of our grief, whatever its source. She is utterly uncompromising about it:

> *When grief sits with you, its tropical heat*
> *thickening the air, heavy as water*
> *more fit for gills than lungs;*
> *when grief weights you like your own flesh*
> *only more of it, an obesity of grief,*
> *you think,* How can a body withstand this?

The *tropical heat thickening the air, grief heavy as water more fit for gills than lungs, an obesity of grief filling you up and weighing you down* — these images assault my senses, slip under my skin. I feel claustrophobic, I gasp for air, for light, for space: How could anyone withstand this? Withstand a sorrow that fills every pore, every crevice of mind and body, with sorrow, inconsolable and final?

I have lived through the deaths of my parents and several dear friends; more than once I have left behind a life and a world that I cherished, and more than once I have parted from a partner I loved. But nothing in my experience descends to the heat and pressure of grief described in this poem; nothing except perhaps the time when I was thirty years old and fell hopelessly and helplessly in love with the wife of a colleague.

I, too, was married at the time, and my wife of just three months was pregnant. No, it wasn't pretty; it was the perfect scenario for our world to come crashing down about us. We had all known each other for several years, four of which we had shared a flat in London. There had never been a hint of mutual attraction between my colleague's wife and me, until one day we happened to meet each other's gaze across a room full of friends. The shock, a bolt so strong it sent the whole room reeling, was instant and mutual. From that moment on, and for several months after, we were constantly aware of each other's presence, night and day, wherever we were. We told our partners almost immediately, didn't act on it, and did all we could to keep our connection in check while acknowledging the truth of it. In a few months it became obvious that we would have to separate our lives, and my wife and I moved away from London. It was ten years before the woman and I met again, and by that time our lives had gone their own ways, leaving a trail of tears in their wake.

The last time I saw her before I left London, I felt a weight approaching an "obesity of grief." When I pay attention to it, I can still feel the sensation that I wrote about in my journal at the time, of a metal lid closing over my heart, of my legs feeling encumbered with gravity, of the air having been sucked out of me. My lifeblood had drained away, and for a year or two I was running on empty.

Only then, as Bass says, only when you are utterly defeated by something greater than yourself, only when you cry out in despair and surrender, only then can you

hold life like a face
between your palms, a plain face

I was not ready to hold the future in my hands, not able to know that a greater love was being asked of me — a love not of one woman alone but of life as it was. But then the moment came when I had no choice. There was nothing else to do. When that moment comes, you are willing to hold the face of life in your hands, whatever it looks like — even if it's

a plain face,
no charming smile, no violet eyes

There was nothing charming about the life that awaited me, except of course the imminent birth of my son. The bond with my wife had been seriously weakened; I had no obvious work prospects, having had to leave without notice the organization that my colleague and I were heading up; and the woman I felt intimately and inextricably bonded with was banished from my sight. Yet something in me knew there was only one course of action, which was to bow to the inevitable with as much grace as I could muster.

But that realization did not mean I could simply embrace the life opening before me with open arms and a wide-open heart and move on. The lid over my heart made its presence felt for a long time afterward. Bowing to fate did not make the sorrow dissolve. The sorrow was itself an intrinsic part of the life that I was being given.

In an interview for *Poets & Writers* magazine, Ellen Bass stated, "Writing poetry for me was one of the primary ways that I grieved [for my mother]. I found that working with the poems was more natural to me than any other outward rituals or ceremonies around her death. I just thought during that whole period how fortunate I was to be a poet. I don't know what people do who don't have a way to sit with their experience in a tangible way."

She went on to say, "The essence of writing poetry, for me, is really a way to accept what life brings. That's so hard to do in the living — to really see all that comes to us, both what we want and what we don't want, in some way as equally valuable. In poetry I feel I get the chance to do that. That's what's really the deepest pull."

I suspect that E. E. Cummings used poetry in a similar way: to help him accept the unacceptable. Cummings wrote a heartbreaking love poem called "it may not always be so; and I say." His lover had just left him for someone else, and in this poem Cummings says that if this is really so, then

> *send me a little word;*
> *that i may go unto him,and take his hands,*
> *saying,Accept all happiness from me.*

Such generosity of spirit is rare indeed, and yet Cummings shows that it is possible. The loss of his lover was no easier for him than it is for anyone else. He suffered, however generous his gesture toward his lost love and her new lover. He ends the poem with these two heartbreaking lines:

> *Then shall i turn my face,and hear one bird*
> *sing terribly afar in the lost lands.*

Grief and loss are a kind of death, and death and love are always and ever twins. We are here to love. We cannot help ourselves, whether we love a person or an animal or the sunset or trees or the planet or our family or our country. The more we love, the richer our life experience and the more the world is blessed by our presence. Yet the more we love, the deeper the sorrow when everything we love passes away, and all too soon. If we love, we suffer. Bass's poem reminds us that the only way out of that suffering is through it. We will be brought low by it, softened by it, opened by it, and ushered finally into a love still greater, a love for our own exquisite and painful life as we experience it day by day.

How tender, how strong we are. Being human fills me with gladness. It fills me with sorrow. And Bass's poem fills me with pride, pride that in our humanness we can drink the full draft of our life and emerge more than just who we thought we were.

3.

THE QUARREL

by Conrad Aiken

Suddenly, after the quarrel, while we waited,
Disheartened, silent, with downcast looks, nor stirred
Eyelid nor finger, hopeless both, yet hoping
Against all hope to unsay the sundering word:

While all the room's stillness deepened, deepened about us
And each of us crept his thought's way to discover
How, with as little sound as the fall of a leaf,
The shadow had fallen, and lover quarreled with lover;

And while, in the quiet, I marveled — alas, alas —
At your deep beauty, your tragic beauty, torn
As the pale flower is torn by the wanton sparrow —
This beauty, pitied and loved, and now forsworn;

It was then, when the instant darkened to its darkest, —
When faith was lost with hope, and the rain conspired
To strike its gray arpeggios against our heartstrings, —
When love no longer dared, and scarcely desired:

It was then that suddenly, in the neighbor's room,
The music started: that brave quartette of strings
Breaking out of the stillness, as out of our stillness,
Like the indomitable heart of life that sings

When all is lost; and startled from our sorrow,
Tranced from our grief by that diviner grief,
We raised remembering eyes, each looked at other,
Blinded with tears of joy; and another leaf

Fell silently as that first; and in the instant
The shadow had gone, our quarrel became absurd;
And we rose, to the angelic voices of the music,
And I touched your hand, and we kissed, without a word.

HEARTSTRINGS

"The Quarrel" shows us how a poem can open our eyes to a new way of seeing, and living, the ordinary events of our lives. It is one of the qualities that I most appreciate about poetry — its redemptive treatment of a mundane situation that any of us can see ourselves in. It takes a small, common experience, fills it with successive layers of feeling, and ends with a lyrical, often philosophical, turn. It shows us that a conflict of any kind can be resolved when something of a higher moral and aesthetic frequency enters the scene. Conrad Aiken, I believe, was quite justified in avoiding military service during World War I, claiming that, as a poet, he was part of "an essential industry."

Poetry is indeed an essential industry — essential to civilization, necessary for the fullness of human life. Aiken was not religious, but he said once that he aspired to "a poetic comprehension of man's position in the universe, and of his potentialities as a poetic shaper of his own destiny, through self-knowledge and love."

Aiken was just nine years old when he decided to be a

poet. In that same year his father, a brilliant but unstable Harvard-trained surgeon, had him witness an eye operation, a traumatic experience that recurs in his writings. Much worse followed. When Aiken was eleven his father shot his mother dead and then committed suicide. The event is described in Aiken's autobiographical novel, *Ushant*: "After the desultory early-morning quarrel, came the half-stifled scream, and then the sound of his father's voice counting three, and the two loud pistol shots and he tiptoed into the dark room, where the two bodies lay motionless, and apart, and, finding them dead, found himself possessed of them forever."[5]

That quarrel, of course, is not the one described in his poem. Aiken was married three times, and the catalyst for the poem, which was an early one, was probably an incident between him and his first wife, Jessie McDonald, whom he married in 1912 when he was twenty-three.

Like all great poems, "The Quarrel" acts on us not only through its content — what it has to say — but also through how it is said. When in his later years W. B. Yeats revised some of his early poems, many of his friends were aghast. In response he writes:

The friends that have it I do wrong

Whenever I remake a song,
Should know what issue is at stake:

It is myself that I remake.[6]

Yeats is declaring that poetry is a moral act. It aims to restore the uprightness of the self — first, the poet's self, and then by extension, the reader's. This is what Aiken achieves in "The Quarrel." Yeats goes on to say, "How hard is that purification from insincerity, vanity, malignity, arrogance, which is the discovery of style."

Style, then, for Yeats, was the vehicle for the moral act of poetry. Conrad Aiken, who won the Pulitzer Prize in 1930 for his *Selected Poems*, was known as a master of style, perhaps most admired for his exploration of the music within poetic forms. You can hear in "The Quarrel" how the lines are deliberately melodic, varied in rhythm, with the second and fourth line of each stanza rhyming. Some critics have complained that this formality kept his gaze looking back to the Victorian era rather than looking forward to modernism; and it's true that, like his great friend T. S. Eliot, Aiken admired the rigor and exactitude of earlier poetic styles. When you remember Yeats's assertion, though — that style is a means of purifying one's own insincerity and ignorance — you realize that Aiken's formalism serves a greater end. "The Quarrel" does not contain a single false note. Its aim is precisely to restore the uprightness of the self in the midst of adversity, and its music plays to that end.

One nineteenth-century voice Aiken admired enormously was Emily Dickinson's, so much so that he edited *Selected Poems of Emily Dickinson* (1924) and was largely responsible for establishing her posthumous literary reputation.

In Dickinson, with her fastidiousness in finding the exact right word, Aiken had a rare and exalted mentor.

Just one example will serve to illustrate. On the original sheet of one of her poems, Dickinson had put thirteen adjectives in the margin near a line in which she had left a space. The poem is about the need for a preacher to bring alive his Bible stories for an audience of young boys. With a space for the missing word, the line was:

> *Had but the tale a ___ Teller*

The adjectives in the margin were not synonyms. They each attempted to grasp a different aspect of the missing quality of the preacher. Some of the words were *winning, friendly, mellow, hearty, ardent,* and *breathless*. What is it, fundamentally, that will attract an audience to a tale? Dickinson finds the answer not in the *matter* of the sermon, but in the *manner*. She settled on the word *warbling*. The nightingale warbles. Orpheus warbles. Shakespeare warbles — his linguistic music charms the audience. The clergyman must warble, too.

Conrad's "The Quarrel" warbles. Its song lifts you from stanza to stanza, ending in a soft crescendo of "angelic voices." It begins with waiting, with a pause after the storm. Most of us have known the awkwardness of the silence that follows a quarrel.

> *Disheartened, silent, with downcast looks, nor stirred*
> *Eyelid nor finger, hopeless both*

This awkwardness keeps our eyes from each other. The air goes out of our lungs, even out of the room. Any movement can feel awkward, freighted as it is with self-consciousness, like moving through sludge, or fog,

> *hoping*
> *Against all hope to unsay the sundering word*

It's too late, though, to bite your tongue; the words have already flown, and you can only suffer now the weight of them in the air. "Unsay the sundering word": what may in another context seem like outdated phrasing here adds not only to the alliterative lilt of the poem but also to the formality and gravity of the moment.

How did this happen? How did we get here? It's like that, isn't it? Suddenly we are at odds, and we don't know why or how. The offending word may have seemed insignificant in the saying of it, yet it came trailing dark clouds from over some unnoticed horizon. It had a tone, an insinuating inflection, perhaps, that we were unaware of, an echo of some previously undigested pain lost to our conscious memory. And so

> *with as little sound as the fall of a leaf,*
> *The shadow had fallen*

Aiken's image from nature adds to the atmosphere of lyrical melancholy in the poem. This, after all, is not just any quarrel; it is a quarrel between lovers, and all the more poignant because of that. All the more prone, too, to misunderstanding, since a lover more than anyone stirs our shadows to life.

> *I marveled — alas, alas —*
> *At your deep beauty, your tragic beauty, torn*
> *As the pale flower is torn by the wanton sparrow —*

His lover's beauty is made tragic by the shadow that has fallen across it. Tragedy is always the story of the great who have fallen. His lover's beauty is deep because it is more than skin-deep; it must surely be a beauty of soul that the poet sees — and at the very moment that it appears lost to him. Aiken highlights in a few words the ironic and tragic truth that we often only truly value something or someone just as we are about to lose it or her. Again, Aiken uses a searing image from nature to plant the scene in our imagination rather than simply leaving it at the superficial level of information that the rational mind can recognize. The flower is "pale" and the sparrow is "wanton," an old term meaning "unprovoked" or "deliberate." I suspect that he is the sparrow and has realized his transgression, one that has made his lover turn pale. In that moment Aiken's sky darkens to midnight, and any hope of reconciliation seems lost.

Most likely you have your own experience of feeling that a relationship is over, when you feel — too late, perhaps — the full weight of all that you are losing. Aiken's lines remind me of Cavafy's poem "The God Abandons Antony" — another poem in which music plays a large part — and the moment I read it just after my wife, Maria, and I finally parted in 2006. Antony and Cleopatra have lost their cherished city of Alexandria. Antony has also lost the protection of his personal deity, Dionysus, god of wine and music. Cavafy urges him to go to the window and listen to the beautiful music of a procession as it passes in the street — to listen, without excuses or denial, knowing that this is what he is losing. To listen

> *To the exquisite music of that strange procession,*
> *And say goodbye to her, to the Alexandria you are losing.*

Reading those lines a few days after we had agreed to end our marriage was like undoing the button of a tight suit. Soon afterward I visited Maria, sat down on the sofa with her, and read Cavafy's poem to her. I wanted her to know that I could feel the richness of all I was losing, that I would not want to diminish our life together by suggesting she didn't matter to me, that I would always recognize and feel grateful for the gifts she had brought into my life. How could I not? And yet we were already gone from each other.

It seems that the couple in "The Quarrel" are already gone from each other, too:

> *When faith was lost with hope*

But it's then, when all seems lost, that Aiken startles the imagination and, beginning with an image that combines the associative power of both nature and music, leads us to a different outcome:

> *the rain conspired*
> *To strike its gray arpeggios against our heartstrings, —*

Heartstrings is very close to *harp strings.* The word *arpeggio* comes from the Italian word *arpeggiare,* which means "to play a harp," which is done by playing one note after another rather than producing an unbroken chord, as when you strum a guitar. The sound of the rain has entered the silence of the room, and to the poet it seems the whole world now is playing down the scale, echoing the feelings of loss in his own heart.

And yet, and yet; though love no longer dared say or do anything, still less hope for anything, still a sliver of desire remains, a desire for a paradise seemingly lost forever, the paradise of lovers in love. If that sliver had not survived, then he would never have heard the music that starts up in the neighbor's room, never have heard it in the way he does then. Music, which has been implicit all the way through in Aiken's sonorous lines, now bursts to the surface, messenger of the gods, "indomitable heart of life," to herald a new world, a new beginning:

> *Tranced from our grief by that diviner grief*

Aiken infers here a sorrow greater than any individual sorrow; "the still, sad music of humanity," Wordsworth calls it. Music spans all the worlds. It can lift us out of our narrowly personal story into the greater love story of humanity, bring us to a humbling kinship with the joyous and sorrowful journey of the human race through time. In that moment, no longer bound by the story we were lost in a moment before, we can raise "remembering eyes," and then, only then, the shadow gone, can "our quarrel" become "absurd."

Then and only then can we risk letting ourselves be touched by each other, hand and lips and especially heart once more. The body speaks its language, and words have no need even to form their sounds in the mind. Music raises us to this higher lovemaking. Music alone can give voice to what the loving body knows. How, then, can we not turn to Shakespeare, and his immortal line?:

If music be the food of love, play on.

4.

CUTTING LOOSE

by William Stafford

For James Dickey

Sometimes from sorrow, for no reason,
you sing. For no reason, you accept
the way of being lost, cutting loose from
all else and electing a world
where you go where you want to.

Arbitrary, a sound comes, a reminder
that a steady center is holding
all else. If you listen, that sound
will tell where it is, and you
can slide your way past trouble.

Certain twisted monsters
always bar the path — but that's when
you get going best, glad to be
lost, learning how real it is
here on the earth, again and again.

LISTEN FOR THE SOUND

James Dickey, to whom this poem is dedicated, once commented that William Stafford seemed able to say amazing things in his poems without raising his voice, as though he were "murmuring."[7] When asked if he ever felt tempted to speak more loudly, Stafford said he saw no reason. In "Cutting Loose" Stafford murmurs deep truths about being human that people like me need a whole essay to delve into.

Take that first sentence, for example, so easy to slide over:

Sometimes from sorrow, for no reason,
you sing.

Folded among those few words are centuries of human beings raising their voices in lamentation. The line evokes the mood of the old spirituals — "O Mary, don't you weep, don't you mourn" — the searing agony of the blues, the laments of country music, the book of Lamentations in the Old Testament, and all the spiritual longing that fuels so much of

Middle Eastern and Indian music. All over the world people have cried out in their grief, their loss, their sorrow, through song.

And as Stafford knows, the songs burst forth for no reason. Far from diminishing or singing away the sorrow, a song is a spontaneous outburst, an outpouring of deep emotion, lifting the singer out of herself and the confines of her personal pain to join a larger sorrow, one that has been weeping in the human heart since time began.

And in doing so, a song can transform personal sorrow into something approximating joy, as if the song itself were a kind of alchemical retort. The Portuguese have a tradition of song called *saudade*, which has been described as "a pleasure you suffer, an ailment you enjoy." The Spanish have their own soulful equivalent in flamenco.

We cry out in our own wilderness, too, when we have lost our way, and these cries also have no reason, no purpose beyond themselves. They bow to our condition; they release us to the reality of what is so: we are lost. We may always have been lost and not realized it. Or we have sensed that we were lost all along but turned the other way, thinking it would be less painful and surely more productive to get on with the business of living.

For me being lost always came with the feeling that something had been missing, like having a hole in my middle that nothing could fill. I spent the earlier years of my adult life trying to fill it with what I felt was meaningful activity: working for nonprofits, writing socially responsible articles for *The*

Guardian, sitting with wise men in India and the West, and so on. The trouble was, no matter what I did, I continued to feel that I did not know what I was meant to be doing or what I was here for. Nothing outside ever filled the nothing inside.

What I did not do in those years was to fully accept the feeling of being lost and empty, to look it in the eye and accept it for my reality. When we do that, I discovered, the scales finally fall from our eyes and we experience profound relief.

Yet Stafford may well have been implying a far simpler sense of loss than the existential angst that I labored through. He may have been thinking of being lost for words before the blank page that confronted him every morning when he sat down to his daily writing session — a discipline he maintained religiously for fifty years. In his acceptance speech for the National Book Award in 1963, he said that the poet "has to be willing to stay lost until what he finds — or what finds him — has the validity that the instant (with him as its sole representative) can recognize — at that moment he is transported, not because he wants to be, but because he can't help it. Out of the wilderness of possibility comes a vine without a name, and his poem is growing with it."

"The wilderness of possibility," whether it is the blank page or feeling directionless, the loss of our bearings in the face of what seems like a great empty space, is disorienting and bewildering. Yet an exhilarating freedom comes in surrendering to the reality of our life as it is in the moment. In being willing to stay lost until found by the poem that wants to be written, Stafford says, there comes a moment when the writer is transported, and out of the wilderness a vine grows without a name.

Kim Stafford said a friend told him his father's "imagination was tuned to the moment when epiphanies were just about to come into being." Stafford's son went on to say that "at such a moment, ambition could be fatal to what we seek. Take a deep breath and wait. What seeks *you* may then appear."[8] It's the same with life, Stafford says in "Cutting Loose."

When we surrender to being lost, a sense of freedom emerges — freedom from the need to keep a tight rein on our life, freedom from the need to *know*. Perhaps Stafford is pointing to this when he speaks of

> *cutting loose from*
> *all else and electing a world*
>
> *where you go where you want to.*

When we cut loose from all else except the reality of feeling lost, the world opens up to become a wilderness of possibility, daunting and exhilarating at the same time. Then the one who is eventually prompted to move forward, in the next moment or the next year, is not the familiar identity that bears our name but "a steady center [...] holding all else."

The shift from outer to inner identity may seem simple, but it is not always easy. Rosemerry Trommer wrote a wry poem called "On Forgetting a Line while Memorizing William Stafford's Poem 'Cutting Loose'" that probably speaks for most of us:

> *But cutting loose*
> *from all else? What would those*
> *scissors look like? Imagine the size*
> *of the blades. Snip. My house. Snip.*
>
> *My family. Snip. My voice. My face.*
> *My name. And then in come*
> *the tiny scissors to cut the invisible*
> *inner strands. Snip. My convictions.*
> *Snip. My ambitions. Snip. My talents*
>
> *My dreams. Snip. Snip. With my lips, I say*
> *I want to be cut loose. Meanwhile I wrap*
> *myself in layer on layer on layer*
> *of silken straitjackets and gossamer*
> *shoulds.*

Trommer is not alone in her anxiety, the anxiety of the conscious self who does not want to disappear, however spiritually advisable it might be. Yet Stafford implies that this is simply a case of mistaken identity. We are not who we think we are. A sound that lies beneath all our thinking continues through all our days. If it has any name at all, it would be the sound of silence. It is far closer to who we are than the one who turns when our name is called. Stafford assures us that all will be well if we listen for the sound that seems to come out of nowhere, "arbitrary," and that will lead us to firmer ground.

If you listen, that sound

will tell you where it is and you
can slide your way past trouble.

The steady center this sound leads to was at the heart of Stafford's life experience. It is a compass he refers to throughout his work. In another poem, "The Way It Is," he says:

There's a thread you follow. It goes among
things that change. But it doesn't change [...]
Tragedies happen; people get hurt
or die; and you suffer and get old.
Nothing you do can stop time's unfolding.
You don't ever let go of the thread.

Human beings live at the intersection of time and timelessness. As long as we are alive and living in time, we can be sure that troubles will come. But if we can keep hold of that thread — if we can follow the sound of the "steady center" that doesn't change, even as life around it is in constant motion — then we will be rooted in the timeless, the dimension of our being in which all is already well. Then, as Stafford writes in "Any Morning," we can be content

Just lying on the couch and being happy.
Only humming a little, the quiet sound in the head.

Trouble is busy elsewhere at the moment, it has
so much to do in the world. [...]

Later in the day you can act like the others.
You can shake your head. You can frown.

This, from a poet who grew up in Depression-era Kansas, whose father could not find work. Of those early years, Stafford says,

> We were living partly on what I could earn selling papers and so on, but so far as I could tell that was what being a human being was. I don't know how to get this directly and simply enough, but if you think about it, lots of human beings don't have a job, lots of human beings work in the sugar-beet fields, which I did. There are a lot of happy people working in sugar-beet fields. And I was one of them. You know, you could always crawl into the shade. You had lunch, maybe a peanut-butter-and-jelly sandwich — delicious. The feeling of being alive and relishing your food and drink and company is available anywhere.[9]

Stafford seems to have been born with the gift of this generous view, with a deep sense of gratitude for the simple fact of being alive and being able to see, hear, taste, and touch the richness of the everyday world. His poems are intimate songs of praise for the beauty and the innocence that thrives in the midst of a world of suffering — a beauty and innocence that appear when our hands follow that thread, when our inner ear hears that sound.

Our path will always be strewn with broken branches and stones, yet even the obstacles in our way are part of the path. They make it real. We are not angels, and the hard edges of the physical world offer a resistance that, if they do not break us first, can temper the soul and open it to another world, which is nowhere if not here. This is the world, the seeing, that William Stafford's poetry springs from.

This life is "a vale of Soul-making," Keats says. When we see it that way, being lost is not only part of the journey; it is the royal way to becoming real, meaning that our outer knowing can be an accurate reflection of our inner knowing, "the steady center." That's why Stafford says that we can even be glad to be lost.

Stafford died of a heart attack in Lake Oswego, Oregon, on August 28, 1993, having written a poem that morning containing the lines:

> *"You don't have to*
> *prove anything," my mother said. "Just be ready*
> *for what God sends."*

He was in touch with that unceasing sound to the very end.

5.

RAIN LIGHT

by W. S. Merwin

All day the stars watch from long ago
my mother said I am going now
when you are alone you will be all right
whether or not you know you will know
look at the old house in the dawn rain
all the flowers are forms of water
the sun reminds them through a white cloud
touches the patchwork spread on the hill
the washed colors of the afterlife
that lived there long before you were born
see how they wake without a question
even though the whole world is burning

ORIGINAL WONDER

"Rain Light" shimmies its way through my senses and leaves in its wake a glimmer of wonder that shines in my mind long after I have put the poem down and moved on with my day. Buttering some toast, feeding the dog, walking outside — whatever I do, a trace lingers of the original wonder that W. S. Merwin summons in this remarkable poem.

It is a wonder that we are here at all. It is a wonder that the stars insinuate their light into our birth and our life and shine into us whenever we drop the veils that so often cloud our eyes. It is a wonder that "the flowers are forms of water," that everything in this living world is not only connected but inherently and forever inseparable. It is a wonder, too, that our lives are infused with memory, and that our memories swell into nostalgia, the original meaning of which is homecoming.

Merwin's poem comes trailing the savor of homecoming, not just to a particular hillside or house or intimacy with his mother, but to the preciousness of living on this planet at this time, a time when the natural world, which has seemed eternal to countless generations, is itself in danger of dissolving, the poles and the species, the flora and fauna. For someone like Merwin, a lifelong environmentalist and passionate advocate for the natural world, this dissolution is visceral.

Yet he is not preaching a sermon here or warning about what may come if we do not heed the signs. "Rain Light" doesn't have a message; rather, it conveys an inchoate feeling that seeps up between the lines and generates the sensation, the thrill, even, of wonder. The rational mind does not warm to wonder. What does warm to it is another deeper and sometimes less accessible faculty, which Merwin and many before him, not least Wordsworth and Coleridge, call imagination. For Merwin, it is not our intellect or intelligence that makes us uniquely human; it is the imagination. The imaginal world is seamless. Everything is of a piece, even if it doesn't make sense. And "Rain Light" makes no obvious sense to the conscious, thinking mind. Merwin himself has said, in an interview with Terry Gross on *Fresh Air*, that he himself doesn't quite know what it is about.

This is a poem that, while made of words, you cannot quite put into words. It's not a poem to understand but to feel. That is what Merwin meant, I think, when he said he didn't know what it was about. All we can do is try on different words for what remains after we read it, a sensation, a shift in the air, a shimmer in the body.

Though I have used the word *wonder* in describing "Rain Light," the poem's flavor seeps out even beyond wonder. *Mystery* is a word we could use, and in reading we may sense we are as much a mystery to ourselves as the poem is to us — in which case the poem will have done its work, even as we do not know what that work is. *Loss* is another word we could use, and the poem is full of the poignancy of it: the loss of the poet's mother, the loss of the past, the loss of innocence in a world gone awry. Yet tenderness is there as well to adumbrate the loss, the tenderness of knowing that nothing and no one, least of all ourselves, is separate from anyone or anything else, a knowing that transcends death and dissolution itself. Someone you love dies, and the stars go on. Something beyond each of us endures even when, as the poem's last line says, the whole world is burning.

The poet's mother can assure him then that he will be all right, come what may, that

> *whether or not you know you will know*

Those lines sound paradoxical, and they are, but they are speaking to two different kinds of knowing, that of the intellect and that of the heart. Merwin may or may not know intellectually, his mother says, but something in him will know that he will be all right. That something is the intelligence of the heart, a felt sense that communicates not in words but in quiet, in stillness. We can know this, too, when we are present to ourselves, however much the outward circumstance of our life and the world may suggest the contrary.

"Rain Light" is all paradox. Everything dissolves and yet nothing disappears. Paradox confounds conventional wisdom, our rational intelligence, which tells us the answers we think we need to know, how the world is, and how we can navigate it. Paradox speaks to our imagination. It awakens us to a different order of being, one in which both/and replaces either/or. It implies a world in which the dark and the light are inherent aspects of a unified field of being.

We can only embrace paradox with the intelligence of the heart, which rests in the knowing of our inherent insepara-bility from all life, whatever happens. The mind separates; the heart unifies.

Merwin's mother shows him this by pointing to the flow-ers, which are forms of water fructified by the sun and which have emerged year upon year on the hillside. They transcend time this way, as everything transcends its own dissolution by joining with the wind and the stars and the softness of the earth. Energy is indestructible, and nothing ever goes any-where, his mother seems to be saying.

Even though the whole world is burning

she tells Merwin, you will be all right. He will be all right if he rests in the heart's intelligence, not in the mind's restless search for answers and absorption in argument. Yet being all right does not mean that we don't need to respond to the crises and calamities of the world. It doesn't mean not caring for this earth, this world of human beings, animals, and red-woods. After all, the world is burning. No, it means you hold the big picture along with your private one, your hope along with your tears. It means that even while doing all you can to do no harm, you hear the echo of Merwin's mother's words, a heartbeat in the chest.

Amy Gerstler, in the *Los Angeles Times*, called Merwin "a channeler of ancient paradoxes; a post-Presbyterian Zen poet." Zen practitioner he is, and has been for decades. Post-Presbyterian he is, too, for his father was a Presbyterian minister, one who forbade music and dancing in the family house. Merwin happily shook off his father's influence early on, and his poetry, especially his later writings, sings its music without even the hindrance of punctuation.

Except for the third line, the lines of "Rain Light" all have nine syllables, and the sustained harmony casts a spell, as all great poems do, that takes the reader into a state resembling a waking dream. In this porous state we can receive the wisdom we have no words for. Philip Sidney, in his *Apology for Poetry*, says that poetry begins in delight and ends in wisdom. That delight is what Merwin's music brings. It is an enchantment, like Ariel's music in *The Tempest*, leaving us more clear-eyed and yet paradoxically more filled with delight than we were a moment before.

When people say they are intimidated by poetry or do not understand it, it is likely because the delight has gone out of the lines. And the more we merely read a poem on the page rather than hear it, the more its delight will escape us. A poem's sound and rhythm reach our breastbone via the human voice, our own or anyone else's; until the voice brings them alive, the words on the page risk merely being read in two dimensions. This is the difference between poetry and prose.

Merwin's own love of poetry came from hearing it read aloud when he was a child. He would hear the King James translation of the Psalms, hear hymns in his father's church, hear his mother read Tennyson. Merwin relates the creative act itself to hearing. He has said that he hears a poem rather than thinks it up. He does not know where a poem comes from but rather sits down every day and makes himself available to what, for centuries, has been known as the muse. Wonder and mystery are an intrinsic part of the creative act of writing poetry.

Ultimately, so is love, and at heart "Rain Light" is a love poem, a love poem to all that lives and breathes; to the past, present, and future, however dark the present may seem. In his poem "Love," Czesław Miłosz says,

> *Love means to learn to look at yourself*
> *The way one looks at distant things*
> *For you are only one thing among many.*
> *And whoever sees that way heals his heart,*
> *Without knowing it, from various ills —*
> *A bird and a tree say to him: Friend.*

For Miłosz, love means nonattachment, in the sense of seeing one's own life from the larger perspective of all life, knowing it to be just one part of a much larger story. Paradoxically, this nonattachment is the most intimate way of being we can know, so much so that a bird and a tree say to us, "Friend." We do what we can, and we let go. This is the love that invisibly courses its way through "Rain Light."

6.

HOW THE LIGHT COMES

by Jan Richardson

I cannot tell you
how the light comes.

What I know
is that it is more ancient
than imagining.

That it travels
across an astounding expanse
to reach us.

That it loves
searching out
what is hidden,
what is lost,
what is forgotten

or in peril
or in pain.

That it has a fondness
for the body,
for finding its way
toward flesh,
for tracing the edges
of form,
for shining forth
through the eye,
the hand,
the heart.

I cannot tell you
how the light comes,
but that it does.
That it will.
That it works its way
into the deepest dark
that enfolds you,
though it may seem
long ages in coming

or arrive in a shape
you did not foresee.

And so
may we this day
turn ourselves toward it.
May we lift our faces
to let it find us.
May we bend our bodies
to follow the arc it makes.
May we open
and open more
and open still
to the blessed light
that comes.

THE LIGHT IN THE DARK

Jan Richardson gave this wonderful poem a subtitle, "A Blessing for Christmas," which I am not including because it would make the focus too narrow for the purposes of this book, which is universal in spiritual reach and espouses no particular religious tradition. Richardson is a poet, an artist, and an ordained minister in the United Methodist Church. "How the Light Comes" is in *Circle of Grace*, her collection following the seasons of the Christian year, beginning with Advent.

However, this poem reaches down so deeply into the essence of universal spiritual reality that it lifts our gaze beyond any religious identity to what is always and ever present, always and ever true, however difficult life may seem and however engulfed the world may seem in chaos. The light serves as a metaphor for consciousness, which illumines everything and is neither inside nor outside but everywhere. It is at the heart of every religious tradition, and union with it is the goal of all mystical paths.

Richardson took for her inspiration the Christmas story

as told in the gospel of John, which has none of the usual trappings of a manger, shepherds, angels, and magi. John, the true mystic among all the disciples, whose gospel stands out from the others in its depth of spiritual wisdom, shaves the traditional Christmas story down to just three primordial elements: light, word, and incarnation. He says, "The light shines in the darkness, and the darkness has not overcome it" (1:5) and "I am the light of the world. Whoever follows me will never walk in darkness, but will have the light of life" (8:12).

Out of these lines, and her poet's imagination, Richardson weaves the poem we have here. There is no mention of Christ being the light of the world; rather, the poem's light shines on its own. The poet does not know how it comes — as if we will ever know how it comes, how consciousness begins — but that it does come she is certain, and that it always has been, "more ancient than imagining," receding back, and I would say forward, in time, so much that time itself cannot contain it. Nor can our imagination, our most elastic faculty, so much more versatile and plastic than theology or philosophy, ever begin to picture it. This is what Henry David Thoreau means when he says, "With all your science can you tell me how it is, and whence it is, that light comes into the soul?" The light and the word are beyond science and beyond words, but we do what we can with what we have, and poetry is the best form words can take to express the inexpressible.

In saying that the light loves what is "hidden" and "lost," Richardson suggests that there is nowhere that the light is not, that it finds its way into even the darkest, most sorrowful, and most forgotten corners of existence. In fact, if we return to John, who says "the light shines in the darkness," we can assume that the light is already present in our darkness, as it is already present everywhere in everything. In this sense, the light neither comes nor goes but always is, even though we may not be aware of it, our attention turned, as it often is, to the problems and preoccupations of the day.

The light is everywhere; it is consciousness itself, the presence of awareness that, as Wordsworth says, in "Lines Written a Few Miles above Tintern Abbey," "rolls through all things":

> *The round ocean and the living air,*
> *And the blue sky, and in the mind of man,*
> *A motion and a spirit that impels*
> *All thinking things, all objects of all thought*

Yet the uniquely Christian idea that Richardson emphasizes is "that it has a fondness for the body," which is a beautiful way of implying its incarnation, not only in a singular individual like Jesus but in all of us. We ourselves are the light of the world when our life is guided by that light. When the light shines through our eyes, it illumines everything we see; when it shines through our hands, it infuses everything we touch; and when it shines through our heart, it spreads across the world. The tenth-century Christian mystic Saint Symeon the New Theologian wrote these ecstatic lines in a poem called "We Awaken in Christ's Body":

I move my hand, and wonderfully
my hand becomes Christ, becomes all of Him [...]

I move my foot, and at once
He appears like a flash of lightning.
Do my words seem blasphemous? — Then
open your heart to Him

and let yourself receive the one
who is opening to you so deeply.
For if we genuinely love Him,
we wake up inside Christ's body

where all our body, all over,
every most hidden part of it,
is realized in joy as Him,
and He makes us, utterly, real [...]

(Translated by Stephen Mitchell)[10]

Symeon's awakening, or realization, takes place not in the mind, or even in the heart alone, but throughout the physical being. In these lines Symeon dissolves the schism between body and spirit, mind and heart, this world and any other. It would be difficult to find a more beautiful affirmation of the physical world, so unusual in the more canonical Christian texts and yet so resonant with the Christian promise of broken bodies being made whole, of the transfiguration of Christ. Except the transfiguration San Symeon speaks of takes place not in the historical time of Jesus, or on some future Judgment Day, but here and now for any individual who is able to "genuinely love Him," by which Symeon means able to forget oneself and disappear in that love. To become zero.

San Symeon affirms the embodiment of the light, the living in and as the light; and it has always been, through the centuries, and in every religion, a dangerous claim to make. Al-Hallaj, a tenth-century Persian mystic, was famous for declaring "I am the Truth." The orthodox of the day took him to mean he was God, whereas his Sufi followers understood him to infer a mystical annihilation of the separate ego, allowing him to become one with all things, and claim the unity of consciousness available to everyone. After years of imprisonment, he was eventually executed in 922 on the charge of desecrating the holy shrine in Mecca by saying that "the important thing is to proceed seven times around the Kaaba of one's own heart." Thousands of people witnessed his execution on the banks of the Tigris River in Baghdad. First he was punched in the face by his executioner, then lashed until unconscious, and then decapitated. Witnesses reported that Al-Hallaj's last words under torture were "all that matters for the ecstatic is that the Unique should reduce him to Unity." Among his writings are the lines:

> I saw my Lord with the eye of the heart.
> I asked, "Who are You?"
> He replied, "You."

Mystics of every tradition have had the same realization: that we ourselves are an expression of the light we are looking for.

That light is personal and impersonal at the same time. It is inseparable from world events, however difficult it may be to acknowledge the light hidden within civilization's darkest hours, and it is inseparable, too, from our personal suffering, which is absolved as we surrender to the light that sustains us always. This is not to brush aside the sorrow we may feel for our country, this earth, this world. It is not to bypass the personal pain we feel all too acutely, the pain of a broken body, a broken spirit, a broken will. It is not to resort to the cliché that all suffering contains a hidden gift. Try telling that to someone who has just received a cancer diagnosis. Suffering sucks, but it is true that when we can no longer rely on our personal strength and will, when we cry out or bow down in surrender, the shell around our heart can crack open and let the light come through.

This is what happened to my partner, Breen Jenkins. Her previous partner, of fifteen years, died suddenly from a stroke. She told me,

> One day he was there and the next day he was not and my life was changed forever. I woke up day after day in a thick fog of grief. Every day, merely surviving was almost too much to bear. Never before had I felt the weight of existence like that. One day soon after his departure, in the kitchen, not doing anything, I felt something. A glow, inside my chest. It was as if the

sun had made a sudden appearance, not outside my
window but in my body. I stopped and felt into this
curious phenomenon. The light grew brighter and
more intense. It spread through my body from its
source in the center of my chest, and then the yellow
light glowed outward into the room. This happened
several times in the next few weeks and months. It
seemed that the deeper I fell into my grief without
resistance, the more the light would appear. One day
the light stopped and I woke up and thought, "the
worst is over now." I'm not afraid of pain anymore; I
know that no matter what happens, the real beauty of
life lies in the deepest surrender to the unbearable.[11]

This is what Richardson means when she says that the light

works its way
into the deepest dark
that enfolds you

How might that happen? When, says Richardson, we

turn ourselves toward it.
May we lift our faces
to let it find us. [...]
May we open
and open more
and open still

to the blessed light
that comes.

Her words echo those of San Symeon:

Do my words seem blasphemous? — Then
open your heart to Him

and let yourself receive the one
who is opening to you so deeply.

This opening can never be an act of will. We cannot simply decide to open. Only when we drop the struggle — to be the captain of our own ship, to run our life as we see fit — only then may another way open before us, one whose existence we may never have suspected. Perhaps then we shall see that all along we have been a lamp that has been unaware of its own light.

7.

NOW YOU KNOW THE WORST

by Wendell Berry

To my granddaughters who visited the Holocaust Museum
on the day of the burial of Yitzhak Rabin, November 6th, 1995

Now you know the worst
we humans have to know
about ourselves, and I am sorry,

for I know that you will be afraid.
To those of our bodies given
without pity to be burned, I know

there is no answer
but loving one another,
even our enemies, and this is hard.

But remember:
when a man of war becomes a man of peace,
he gives a light, divine

though it is also human.
When a man of peace is killed
by a man of war, he gives a light.

You do not have to walk in darkness.
If you will have the courage for love,
you may walk in light. It will be

the light of those who have suffered
for peace. It will be
your light.

THERE IS NO "OTHER"

Since the late 1970s, poet, novelist, and environmentalist Wendell Berry has spent his Sunday mornings on solitary walks on his Kentucky farm, observing the world and writing. His Sunday reveries have nurtured a remarkable series of meditative poems, now expanded and collected as *A Timbered Choir: The Sabbath Poems, 1979–1997*. The mood of the poems is prayerlike, and many of the poems, like this one, are an expression of atonement. Berry writes in his preface that he wrote his poems "in silence, in solitude, mainly out of doors," and he hopes they will be read as they were written, "slowly, and with more patience than effort."

The first three lines of this Sabbath poem hit me like a train.

Now you know the worst
we humans have to know
about ourselves, and I am sorry

His granddaughters are visiting a Holocaust Museum, perhaps in DC or Houston or Los Angeles. Perhaps even in Berlin. That same day Yitzhak Rabin was being buried. He had been gunned down in a public square in Tel Aviv by a right-wing fanatic who opposed the Oslo Peace Accords. In 1992 Rabin had been reelected as prime minister on a platform embracing the Israeli-Palestinian peace process. He signed several historic agreements with the Palestinian leadership as part of the Oslo Accords, and in 1994, Rabin won the Nobel Peace Prize, along with longtime political rival Shimon Peres and Palestinian leader Yasser Arafat. In his Nobel Peace Prize lecture, Rabin, who was himself a general and had been in the Israeli military for much of his life, said that "military cemeteries in every corner of the world are silent testimony to the failure of national leaders to sanctify human life."

After his assassination Rabin became a symbol of the potential of the Israeli-Palestinian peace process, despite all the seemingly intractable problems that continue to lie in its way.

It's the phrase "I am sorry" that packs the punch at the end of these three lines. In the museum Berry's granddaughters are following the story of one of the most degrading episodes in human history, a terrifying example of the lowest we human beings can go in our treatment of one another. While they are in the museum, the Israeli who was dedicating his later life and career to peace on behalf of the Jewish nation is buried. The collective tragedy of the Holocaust is amplified now by a specific individual's tragic end. Now Berry's granddaughters know the worst there is to know about humankind, both in general and specific terms.

The only words Berry can find to say to them are "I am sorry." This "sorry" says to me that no words can ever fill the vacuum left by the innumerable people who lost their lives to gratuitous murder and torture, that no gesture can ever wipe away the tears. This "sorry" acknowledges our helplessness in the face of what we humans do to each other. The horror of it leaves us speechless.

I felt the inadequacy of words myself many years ago when I first went through the gates of Dachau concentration camp outside Munich. Standing at the edge of the gas oven, staring into the long huts where thousands of men, women, and children were crammed together before an end many did not know was coming, I felt numb. There were no tears I could cry, no words I could say. There were ashes on my tongue.

There is still more to Berry's "sorry"— an acknowledgment of responsibility. Wendell Berry is sorry for what his generation is bequeathing to the next, and the next. Sorry that his grandchildren have to take this tragic story on as part of their own human story and feel the fear that comes with it. Berry does not separate himself from the perpetrators of evil. He does not say that those people are evil and we, today, in this time and place, are not. We all bear responsibility for the injustices that human beings inflict on fellow human beings. It is a collective failing, ingrained in the human journey through time.

I did not know this all those years ago on that visit to Dachau. I was still in the shock of how people — *those* people — could bring themselves to carry out such orders. It was *they* who perpetrated this, not I; not we. We — the more enlightened, the more civilized, the more immune to the collective fear that always requires a scapegoat — would never stoop to such inhuman acts of degradation and murder. On a vastly different scale, yet in the same inhuman vein, we would never countenance burning down a Planned Parenthood building and everyone in it because we hate what we think it stands for. We would never hunt down immigrants, separate them from their families, and throw them penniless and alone across the border. We would never carry out acts of random violence or a suicide mission to prove our belief in God.

Since my visit to Dachau, I have learned both in my own life and in the flow of our common history that unspeakable atrocity is nothing if not human. No other creature devises such torments. Inhumanity is intrinsic to the human story and so exists as a potential in every one of us. Even stranger is the fact that inhuman acts are undertaken by people who are convinced of the justice of their actions. They act on what they see to be the logical conclusion of a belief they cling to so tightly that there is no daylight between the belief itself and who they think they are, their very identity.

And yet we all hold tightly to beliefs like this, and too often we are so blended with them that they form an intrinsic part of our identity. When these beliefs are challenged or assaulted, it is as if we ourselves are being threatened. Generally we do not go to the extreme of harming others on behalf of a belief, however dear it may be to us. But given fertile conditions — the wrong company, the loss of meaning, a sense of powerlessness, a ripe moment in history — there is no saying what we might do. No culture is exempt from the horror that we all too easily associate with Nazism or Rwanda or Pol Pot or Syria. It could just as easily be the United States, and maybe even soon.

For Wendell Berry there is only one possible answer to the inhumanity that is part of our collective inheritance:

> *To those of our bodies given*
> *without pity to be burned, I know*
>
> *there is no answer*
> *but loving one another*

"Loving one another" can sound as trite as a saying on a bumper sticker. It has been said that it is far easier to love everyone than it is to love one individual. Loving one another, when it stretches no further than a pleasant concept, allows us to stay in abstract generalities rather than getting bruised in the rough and tumble of loving specific individuals. Yet love for others can transcend conceptual understanding and become a lived experience. We might begin by practicing empathy, feeling what it would be like to be someone else, with his pains and fears and longings. The more we can experience someone in this way, the more we feel her humanity and know that it is just like ours, even though the details of her story may be very different. Strangers whose names we will never know can become living individuals in our eyes, people with their own anxieties and joys and aspirations. Their own sad and hopeful life, just like ours.

A friend of mine who lives in Manhattan told me he was on the subway one day sitting opposite a man who was gazing at the floor. The man's two young children were running wildly up and down the carriage, shouting at each other. Finally, my friend could bear it no longer.

"Can't you do something about your children?" he said, glaring at the man.

"Oh, I'm so sorry," the man replied, looking up. "My wife died a few hours ago, and we have just come from the hospital."

Imagine for a moment, if you had complained about his children, how you might have felt on hearing the father's apology. In an instant my friend saw these two annoying children and their father as hurting and vulnerable human beings overwhelmed by their all-too-human grief. In a single moment their sorrow became his sorrow. He went over and sat next to the man. "I am so sorry," he said. What else was there to say? What else can Wendell Berry say in his poem?

In her poem "Kindness," Naomi Shihab Nye says that if we are to know what kindness really is, we must be able to look upon a man dead in the road:

You must see how this could be you,
how he too was someone

who journeyed through the night with plans
and the simple breath that kept him alive.

When we begin to see and feel another human being, she ceases to be an object and instead becomes a subject. The atrocities we have committed against one another throughout history have been possible because the other has been made an object and thus not a living, breathing person. If we turn someone into a something, it becomes easier to abuse or kill him, because in our mind he is not really alive in the way we are. The early American settlers could kill the native peoples with impunity because they believed they had no soul. Slaves shipped from Africa could be treated like animals because they were not considered fully human.

Our practice, then — and it takes practice, because we have been hardwired to sniff out danger in the form of adversaries, the ultimate embodiment of the "other" — is to consciously humanize those people who cross our path, however inhuman their acts may be. It is to look through their actions, without condoning or excusing them, to the lonely self who lives as though separate from the rest of the living universe and feels he can only survive by dominating his environment, both human and natural. Berry acknowledges that our deep humanity calls on us to love

even our enemies, and this is hard.

Very hard indeed. So how to begin? Taha Muhammad Ali, the great Palestinian poet who died in 2011, shows us in his remarkable poem "Revenge." The owner of a souvenir shop, Muhammad Ali lived in Nazareth under Israeli occupation. He says if he could meet the murderer of his father, the man who razed their home and expelled him from his own country, he would challenge him to a duel and take his revenge.

> *But if it came to light,*
> *when my rival appeared,*
> *that he had a mother*
> *waiting for him,*
> *or a father who'd put*
> *his right hand over*
> *the heart's place in his chest*
> *whenever his son was late*
> *even by just a quarter-hour*
> *for a meeting they'd set —*
> *then I would not kill him,*
> *even if I could.*

(Translated by Peter Cole, Yahya Hijazi, and Gabriel Levin)

Nor would he kill him if he discovered the man had brothers or sisters who loved him, or a wife or children, or friends or neighbors or allies from a prison or hospital room. And if he turned out to be

> *cut off like a branch from a tree —*

knowing no one, with no friends or family, he would still not add to the pain of his aloneness but would pass him by without a word, and that would be his only revenge. Muhammad Ali, who had plenty of opportunity to practice what he preached in occupied Palestine, speaks from experience, not from the lofty perch of a philosophical ideal. He exhorts us in "Revenge" to humanize our enemies, to feel them to be just like us, an irreplaceable part of the human family. The man in his poem exemplifies what Wendell Berry means when he says:

> *But remember:*
> *when a man of war becomes a man of peace,*
> *he gives a light, divine*
>
> *though it is also human.*

His Holiness the Dalai Lama shows us how to take that principle and extend it to the whole human family, including those who wish us dead. The Chinese government wants the Dalai Lama dead. They paint him as a devil who is subverting the Chinese state and keeping the Tibetan people in bondage to anachronistic religious beliefs. The Dalai Lama's response to their hatred and lies is to breathe their venom into himself as smoke and black bile, and to return it to them as a stream of love and compassion emanating from his heart. We can practice a layperson's simple form of this by resting our attention in the heart whenever we meet someone and noticing the difference it makes to our conversation.

> *If you will have the courage for love,*
> *you may walk in light.*

Wendell Berry is right. It takes courage to respond from love. It is easy to understand how actions and responses like those of Taha Muhammad Ali or the Dalai Lama take great courage. But we also need courage in overriding our instinctual reactivity and responding with an open heart, even in the most mundane of our daily encounters — the courage not to be always in the right, the courage to go against the habitual drive toward defensiveness and self-justification.

Easy to say, but we all know that it's not always so easy to follow, especially when it seems so dark outside. And yet in the heart of that kind of darkness, just after the World Trade Center attacks, the zoologist Stephen Jay Gould managed to write these beautiful lines in the *New York Times*:

> The tragedy of human history lies in the enormous potential for destruction in rare acts of evil, not in the high frequency of evil people. Complex systems can only be built step by step, whereas destruction requires but an instant. Thus, in what I like to call the Great Asymmetry, every spectacular incident of evil will be balanced by 10,000 acts of kindness, too often unnoted and invisible as the "ordinary" efforts of a vast majority.[...]

In human terms, ground zero is the focal point for a vast web of bustling goodness, channeling uncountable deeds of kindness from an entire planet — the acts that must be recorded to reaffirm the overwhelming weight of human decency. The rubble of ground zero stands mute, while a beehive of human activity churns within, and radiates outward, as everyone makes a selfless contribution, big or tiny according to means or skills, but each of equal worth. [...]

Word spreads like a fire of goodness, and people stream in, bringing gifts from a pocketful of batteries to a $10,000 purchase of hard hats.

This fire of goodness is the visible expression of what stands beyond all notions of right and wrong. And Gould kept faith with this, the human spirit, in spite of all that had just happened on his doorstep in downtown Manhattan. His words reflect a larger, knowing presence than the frightened conditioned self that is so easy to inhabit in the face of darkness, a presence beyond the separate sense of self, one in which we are one body and one mind with everything that lives and breathes. The more we are committed to remembering this, our true and shared identity with all life, the more our fractured world can heal. To be committed to this in whichever way our life allows is to live an engaged spiritual life. It is believing that although there are no guarantees for the future, humanity is worth loving, worth working for, and worth praying for, no matter what.

8.

A BRIEF FOR THE DEFENSE

by Jack Gilbert

Sorrow everywhere. Slaughter everywhere. If babies
are not starving someplace, they are starving
somewhere else. With flies in their nostrils.
But we enjoy our lives because that's what God wants.
Otherwise the mornings before summer dawn would not
be made so fine. The Bengal tiger would not
be fashioned so miraculously well. The poor women
at the fountain are laughing together between
the suffering they have known and the awfulness
in their future, smiling and laughing while somebody
in the village is very sick. There is laughter
every day in the terrible streets of Calcutta,
and the women laugh in the cages of Bombay.
If we deny our happiness, resist our satisfaction,
we lessen the importance of their deprivation.
We must risk delight. We can do without pleasure,

but not delight. Not enjoyment. We must have
the stubbornness to accept our gladness in the ruthless
furnace of this world. To make injustice the only
measure of our attention is to praise the Devil.
If the locomotive of the Lord runs us down,
we should give thanks that the end had magnitude.
We must admit there will be music despite everything.
We stand at the prow again of a small ship
anchored late at night in the tiny port
looking over to the sleeping island: the waterfront
is three shuttered cafés and one naked light burning.
To hear the faint sound of oars in the silence as a rowboat
comes slowly out and then goes back is truly worth
all the years of sorrow that are to come.

IN DEFENSE OF JOY

Who would have thought that we needed a lawyer's brief to defend joy? Jack Gilbert evidently thought so, except he drafts his brief as a resounding poem. He is not alone in thinking that joy needs support in a difficult world. In the novel *Snow*, by Turkish writer Orhan Pamuk, one character says of another that he got drunk so he could resist the happiness rising inside him. The scene is set in the city of Kars, in the far northeast of Turkey. Kars is plunged into snow and ice for months on end. Drunkenness seems to thrive in lands that are cold and dark, perhaps in response to the depression brought on by the intensity and sheer inhospitality of the elements. So Pamuk's suggestion that his character's drunkenness is the result not of depression, but of an uprising of joy, is startling.

On another continent, Wendell Berry wrote something similar:

Why all the embarrassment
About being happy?[12]

Berry's question summons two connected responses. Joy makes us feel light, spontaneous, and free of constraint. That is why happiness can be embarrassing, especially in its deeper form of joy — because our normal social inhibitions and constraints tend to weaken and even fall away. We forget ourselves for a moment, our adult seriousness, the weight of our responsibilities, the problems and tasks that fill our days. The spirit of the child we once were can rise uninhibited. In a moment of self-forgetting, of spontaneous joy, we might make a fool of ourselves. We might say the wrong thing or speak out of turn. Or we might speak the truth that no one wants to hear. So we hold back; we bite our tongue; we want to leave the room and go walk in the woods. Or we get drunk in order to fit in, to conform to the local custom of somewhere like Kars. Or we go red with embarrassment.

Most of us were trained as children to fit in, to hold our tongue, to be on our best behavior. Our natural exuberance was put on a leash and only set loose in culturally condoned outlets like sports. So later in life guilt can arise along with our natural joy, and a feeling that this exuberance ought to be held in check, as it was in our childhood.

In "A Brief for the Defense," Jack Gilbert's main argument in defense of joy is that *We are not guilty, your honor*. We all hear every day how the world is a terrible mess. It always has been, and things do not seem to be getting better. Only the names and the countries change, but the news is always the same. "Sorrow everywhere. Slaughter everywhere." Gilbert hardly has to remind us. Not so long ago it was Bosnia, and then Kosovo. Then it was Rwanda and the Congo. Then it was Aleppo and the thousands of immigrants drowning weekly in the Mediterranean. Then Myanmar. It's always been Palestine. Tomorrow it might be down the street in the town where you live.

What is our responsibility for all this suffering and sorrow? We are all human; we are all essentially one people, whatever the color of our skin — even if it doesn't feel like it sometimes, or even often. Whether or not we can allow it, we are all kin with the people who gave us Trump, and with the Russian pilots who bombed the life out of a Syrian city. So to the degree that our heart is open to it, we all share in the suffering around us. It is not our fault, but it is our responsibility, because we, too, are human. Gilbert's response to the question of collective responsibility is not to say that we should wring our hands and blame ourselves or each other, but to say that "we enjoy our lives because that's what God wants." This is the deeper responsibility that goes along with the responsibility we all bear for the world's suffering.

That doesn't mean we should close our eyes and ears to the tragedies of human existence. It doesn't mean we are not moved to do whatever it befits our character and talents to do. It means that along with whatever actions we take, we have a deeper responsibility: to affirm "what God wants," as the poet says. That is a very large package in just a few small words, and if we are to inhale the full scent and flavor of this poem we would do well to ask the question, Where, for Jack Gilbert, does enjoyment, joy, and true happiness come from? Where

does it come from for you and me? The answer is more cul-
turally determined than we might think.

The response to this question has changed through the
centuries. By mentioning God, Gilbert infers a spiritual qual-
ity to human happiness. His injunction to enjoy this world
rather than waiting for true happiness in the next is a direct
descendant of Luther's protestation that it is foolish to think
it a sin to be happy. On the contrary, for the Protestants, espe-
cially the Anglo-Saxon kind, the experience of happiness on
earth was an outward sign of God's grace. For fifteen hundred
years before the Reformation, happiness had been associated
with the afterlife, this world being a vale of tears whose pre-
vailing image was Christ on the cross.

Gilbert was far from being a churchgoing Protestant, but
he was part of a culture that is so saturated with Protestant
views that it is now, in a postreligious age, easy to forget the
origins of our contemporary attitudes. Yet there are more re-
cent and more pervasive influences than Luther and Calvin
on our notions of happiness. Throughout the seventeenth
century, the Protestant idea that happiness was our natural
state evolved to include the possibility that its presence in our
life might not require God's grace at all; the condition might
occur entirely by natural means. By the eighteenth century
this perspective had evolved to include the belief that hap-
piness was "a self-evident truth." "Does not everyone have
a right to happiness?" asked Abbé Pestré, the author on the
subject in the French encyclopedia of the time. There were
more articles, treatises, and books written on the subject of

happiness in the eighteenth century than in all previous ages combined.

The more discerning minds of the age, such as Samuel Johnson in England and Immanuel Kant in Germany, asked a number of fundamental questions. If happiness is truly a birthright, then how to account for all the misery in the world? Does happiness simply mean feeling good? Fulfilling your desires? Does it imply no more than a balance of pleasure over pain? Was feeling good the same as being good? During the Enlightenment the question, How can I be saved? was largely replaced by the more pragmatic, How can I be happy? The answers to all these questions, Enlightenment thinkers believed, were to be found through human understanding and effort alone.

Inevitably, by its end, the same century in which happiness was asserted to be an earthly goal, and our birthright, also bred new forms of despair. Struggle, difficulty, and failure were as common as ever for even the brightest minds and the most fortunate of people. No matter how hard one worked or how hard one thought, happiness remained elusive. By equating pleasure with the good and seeing all pain to be the presence of evil, Enlightenment thinkers had turned their backs not only on 1,800 years of Christian thought but also on the actual rather than the ideal reality of the majority of human beings. So along came Romanticism and a period of Catholic renewal. Today we might call the Romantics spiritual but not religious. While rarely embracing religious orthodoxies, they did embrace the idea that forces were at work both individually and collectively that were far greater and less evident than reason and will. They also embraced the Christian view that pain was a fact of existence to be accepted and borne — preferably with joy.

Joy is a central and recurring theme in the Romantic vocabulary. For Coleridge, Wordsworth, Byron, Schiller, Emerson, and Whitman, it is not self-created by an act of will or reason, as it was thought to be during the Enlightenment. It is not mere pleasure or an indulgence in earthly delights. Rather, joy constitutes a merging with something greater, more universal, than ourselves, greater than our habitual identity and yet not external to us. God for the Romantics was an internal force. One way of knowing our true identity was to consciously experience and accept our own suffering and the suffering of the world. (Communion with nature was another way.) Bowing to the full truth of our pain allows us to lose our sense of alienation and separateness and know a union in which we are one with all life — not merged with it but one with it. Joy, as Whitman shows us ecstatically in his "Song of Myself," is a highly personal force. And yet to access it, we must connect with the universal joy that animates the world.

Romantic joy echoes closely the perennial spiritual force that some Christians call grace. But Romantic joy is not divinely conferred. It is immanent, dwelling in and as us as it dwells in and as the inherent nature and spirit of the world. It is our true identity, which rather than being constructed asks to be recovered, remembered — a process involving some sacrifice of who we thought we were. That process necessarily involves the pain of releasing illusions and outworn beliefs about ourselves and life. This is the great work that Romanticism asks of those who would take up its challenge. Its promise is of happiness, not in another world but in this one.

Jack Gilbert is a kindred spirit of the Romantics, one who wants to eat the apple whole and take all the consequences. God shows up in many of Gilbert's poems, and angels, and the devil, and he wrestles with all of them. But none of this concerns organized religion. (Gilbert has said that he's not religious, though "it would be a great comfort to believe" if he could.) His spirituality seems, rather, to echo Blake's dictum at the end of *The Marriage of Heaven and Hell*:

> *For every thing that lives is Holy.*

For Gilbert, heaven cannot exist without hell, and both are to be found right here in our lived experience:

> *There is laughter*
> *every day in the terrible streets of Calcutta,*
> *and the women laugh in the cages of Bombay.*

Our happiness, their deprivation — and the other way around — are part of the same cloth. We come close to the holy in the degree that we are able to drink the full draft of life, to swallow the terrible beauty of all of it without blame or rancor.

In a *New York Times* review of Gilbert's collection *The Great Fires*, published in 1994, Patricia Hampl wrote:

> All the desires of a life — especially sexual love, but also the passion for solitude, for poetry itself, for the accuracy of broken vignettes of memory — are understood at last as a single great hunger: "I tried to gnaw my way into the Lord." In these stately yet urgent poems, "the Lord" is the accumulated joys and griefs (and grievances) of a lifetime.
>
> What emerges is divine, whether it is in the Pittsburgh of childhood, under the expatriate sun of the Mediterranean or in the dark Japan of his wife's death. Finally, "God has put off his panoply and is at home with us. / We are returned to what lay beneath the beauty." "Beneath the beauty" are the fullness of life and its culmination, which is not simply loss but death.

In an interview for *The Paris Review*, Gilbert recalled his desire for life, even as a young boy: [I was] "determined not to die until I had lived my life. So much so that I used to pray and make lists. I would say, I know you have to take me away. You have to kill me. But not yet."

Not yet, because desire is Gilbert's engine not his nemesis, and it will pump life into his life to the very last drop, immerse him fully into his life in all its colors, whatever their shade. Gilbert frequently identified in his poems with Orpheus, the poet and musician who wandered his way through the underworld — which is none other than this world. Orpheus sang and celebrated his way along. Gilbert's poems, too, sing and celebrate their way along, through both the darkness and the light.

How does Orpheus know where he is going in the underworld? someone asks in "Orpheus: The Descent," a poem by Edward Hirsch. The answer is "My dearest: by the ache in his left side, / by the echo of sirens pulsing in the distance." Orpheus understands not by seeing, not by being given proof of his direction, but by the faultless compass of his desire-filled heart. This is the compass that Gilbert followed.

We must risk delight. We can do without pleasure,
but not delight. Not enjoyment.

Coleridge could have written those lines. So could have Whitman. Gilbert's delight is not lightweight. He is not talking hedonism here. Rather, he urges the sanctification of our experience by a full immersion in it, whatever it looks like. Full immersion means having our heart in it. It means that our experience, whatever it is, includes the tremors and shocks that only our heart knows. That is why delight is a risk. It can shake us out of our familiar world.

Gilbert followed his star wherever it took him. As a young man, when his first collection was greeted by ecstatic reviews, he tasted celebrity for a while, but he didn't find it interesting for very long. Instead of taking the usual route for a poet of some prestigious academic job, he disappeared for decades in Europe, traveling lightly and mostly broke in France and on the Greek islands. He was never interested in success or failure but rather in the purity of experience, which was the source of his poetic life. A love affair ends, a wife dies, painful and joyful things happen, and the eye of the heart sees them simply, as they are, with full feeling, without judgment.

> *We must admit there will be music despite everything.*

That is none other than Orpheus speaking. To hear the music in the simplest, most ordinary moment, not just in some ecstatic or dreadful event, is what Gilbert dedicated his life to. In the last lines of "A Brief for the Defense," in which he perhaps takes us to the island of Santorini, where he lived for a while, he draws us away from the drama of the images, both heartbreaking and beautiful, that fill much of this poem and brings us with him on a boat as it arrives late at night in a tiny harbor. To be wholly present to what he hears in that moment — it could have been any moment — is enough to redeem a lifetime's sorrow. It is enough to make a life worth living, whatever the cost.

> *To hear the faint sound of oars in the silence as a rowboat*
> *comes slowly out and then goes back is truly worth*
> *all the years of sorrow that are to come.*

9.

IT'S THIS WAY

by Nazim Hikmet

I stand in the advancing light,
my hands hungry, the world beautiful.

My eyes can't get enough of the trees —
they're so hopeful, so green.

A sunny road runs through the mulberries,
I'm at the window of the prison infirmary.

I can't smell the medicines —
carnations must be blooming nearby.

It's this way:
being captured is beside the point,
the point is not to surrender.

(Translated by Randy Blasing and Mutlu Konuk)

WHAT IS A MAN ANYHOW?

This little poem is one great cry of the human spirit, a cry for life, a cry of hope when all seems hopeless. These eleven short lines leave an impression far larger than the single page they stand on, an echo emphatic enough to linger through the centuries. They stand for the green shoot of life that so many have stood by even in the midst of the most terrible sufferings, imprisonments, and deprivations.

Nazim Hikmet spent more than eighteen years as a political prisoner, and his poems were written from deep and harrowing personal experience. Nazim (as he is referred to today in Turkey) was the first and foremost modern poet in the Turkish language and is known as one of the greatest international poets of the twentieth century. Until Nazim picked up a pen, Turkish poetry had for centuries been heavily stylized and effete. He was the first writer to produce poetry in conversational, colloquial Turkish, and although his books were banned for years, he was the first to touch the hearts of ordinary Turks. In his approach to literature and life he was comparable to Walt Whitman, a poet of the common man who scorned conventional patriotism but still insisted that he loved his country beyond all reason.

Nazim was awarded the International Peace Prize in 1950, the same year he gained his release from prison as a result of an international campaign led by Pablo Picasso, Paul Robeson, Bertrand Russell, Pablo Neruda, and Jean Paul Sartre. But he had only been out of prison a few months when he was again forced into exile from Turkey in 1951. He spent the last thirteen years of his life in exile. He died in 1963 in Moscow, where he is buried, although there are moves to return his remains to Turkey.

Nazim grew up in a country that bordered what was then Russia, and that country's revolutionary zeal inspired many Western intellectuals, including Nazim, who paid for his enthusiasm with years in prison in Turkey as a political prisoner. He was outspoken, revolutionary, and a dedicated political activist and communist who was first jailed in 1924 at the age of twenty-two for working on a leftist magazine.

Born in 1902 in Salonika (then part of the Ottoman Empire, now in Greece) where his father was in the foreign service, Nazim grew up in Istanbul. His mother was an artist, and his grandfather, a high-ranking officer, wrote poetry. Through their circle of friends Nazim was introduced to poetry early, publishing his first poems at seventeen. The thread that runs through all his work is an indefatigable affirmation of life, regardless of circumstance.

The first two lines of "It's This Way," which like much of

his work was written in prison, are deceptively unassuming. They carry a simple yet profound philosophy for living:

> *I stand in the advancing light,*
> *my hands hungry, the world beautiful.*

For Nazim the light is always advancing. He insists on seeing the beauty of the world, and his hands will always be hungry for the touch of it, for intimacy with it. But don't imagine that he was merely a proponent of positive affirmations. He wasn't one to bypass his own sorrow. In his poem "Autobiography," he writes:

> *some people know all about plants some about fish*
> *I know separation*
> *some people know the names of the stars by heart*
> *I recite absences*

In another poem, "Some Advice to Those Who Will Serve Time in Prison," he says:

> *It may not be a pleasure exactly,*
> *but it's your solemn duty*
>   *to live one more day*
>   *to spite the enemy.*
> *Part of you may live alone inside,*
>   *like a stone at the bottom of a well.*
> *But the other part*

> *must be so caught up*
> *in the flurry of the world*
> *that you shiver there inside*
> *when outside, at forty days' distance, a leaf moves.*

(Translated by Randy Blasing and Mutlu Konuk)

Nazim knew what it's like to "live alone inside / like a stone at the bottom of a well." If you are alone in a prison cell for years with only an occasional glimpse of the sky, you know what it's like to live at the bottom of a well. And yet he insists on being so open to a larger vision of life, unconstrained by any physical privation, that his being encompasses the world. His defiant optimism is tested to the core and continues to sing in his poetry. That is only possible, he goes on to say in that same poem — and for ten or fifteen years or as long as necessary —

> *as long as the jewel*
> *on the left side of your chest doesn't lose its luster!*

Nazim points here to something deeper than his everyday identity, which left to its own devices would have been crushed long ago by the pain and suffering he experienced. Tom Waits echoes the poet's sentiment in his song "A Diamond in Your Mind," although Nazim is more specific here — it is the mind in the heart that needs to keep its luster. It does so only by knowing from the inside that we are less ourselves and more a part of everything.

There is one life living us all, which is why Walt Whitman could say in "Song of Myself,"

What is a man anyhow? what am I? what are you?

All I mark as my own you shall offset it with your own[…]

> *My foothold is tenon'd and mortis'd in granite,*
> *I laugh at what you call dissolution,*
> *And I know the amplitude of time.*

This is why Nazim can feel such kinship with the green of the trees, the sunny road, and the burgeoning mulberries, even though he is not only in prison but sick in the infirmary. It's why for him the scent of carnations is stronger than the smell of the medicine cabinet. It's why in my own life I could see and feel my common human kinship with the Iranian interrogators who held me captive for a few days in Tehran in 2009; why, far from blaming them, I felt a warmth of compassion both for myself and for them for finding ourselves in that situation together. (The story of my interrogation is told in detail in my book *Dropping the Struggle*.)

The conclusion of Nazim's poem sounds like a struck bell:

> *It's this way:*
> *being captured is beside the point,*
> *the point is not to surrender.*

We can be captured not only by being thrown in prison but by being held hostage in all kinds of daily situations. Our attention can be held captive by an illness, a divorce, loss of livelihood, a death in the family, or any of the other common obstacles that lay across our path. None of them is easy to navigate. Any of them can bring deep sorrow. That, says Nazim, is a given; sorrow comes with being human. But it is not the point. The point is to remember the jewel in the left side of your chest, to remember that life is always bigger than the narrow details of the particular, that

> *The strangest of our powers*
> *Is the courage to live*
> *Knowing that we will die,*
> *Knowing nothing more true.*[13]

10.

ANNUNCIATION

by Marie Howe

Even if I don't see it again — nor ever feel it
I know it is — and that if once it hailed me
it ever does —

and so it is myself I want to turn in that direction
not as toward a place, but it was a tilting
within myself,

as one turns a mirror to flash the light to where
it isn't — I was blinded like that — and swam
in what shone at me

only able to endure it by being no one and so
specifically myself I thought I'd die
from being loved like that.

SOMETHING ELSE CAN SPEAK

Echoing the lines of Nazim Hikmet's poem, Marie Howe said (in an interview with Terry Gross for *Fresh Air*) that "poetry holds the knowledge that we are alive and that we know we are going to die. The most mysterious aspect of being alive might be that, and poetry knows that." Howe's poems bear witness to the great mystery that we are here at all and that all too soon we shall not be.

Her poem "Annunciation" is shot through with the mystery of being. It is one of the most penetrating and awakening poems I have ever read. It leaves me in awe of what is possible for us as human beings. It speaks to the mystery in terms that are themselves both utterly mysterious and yet profoundly familiar, familiar in the sense that we, too, may be visited by some touch of grace from a realm beyond our ordinary experience. "Annunciation" lifts our gaze beyond all difficulty, all trouble, out beyond all moral or ethical standpoints, and brushes us with a grace and wisdom that we know are never really elsewhere yet that are so easily clouded by the sheer weight of living. Annunciation — "the touch of spirit on the body," as Rumi put it — is our inheritance, an everyday miracle that Howe suggests is available anywhere to anyone.

The poem appears in Howe's book *The Kingdom of Ordinary Time*. It is in the section of that book titled "Poems from the Life of Mary." Whatever touched Mary in this poem — and Howe doesn't make this a Bible story; there are no angels, no mention of Christ, and Mary herself is a woman like any woman, her mind absorbed in internal dialogue, in awe of the mystery that just happened to her — whatever it was, its touch was substantial and emphatic enough for her to say,

> *Even if I don't see it again — nor ever feel it*
> *I know it is — and that if once it hailed me*
> *it ever does —*

She knows that the condition of being she glimpsed is constant, always available, and that she needs only to turn toward it rather than waiting for it to bless her again with its presence. She knows it not through some extrasensory faculty or out-of-body or psychotropic experience but through her bodily senses, her sight and touch. Whatever it is, then, is of this world and yet also not of it. Howe echoes the medieval mystic Jacopone da Todi, who writes of love,

> *From five sides You move against me,*
> *Hearing, sight, taste, touch, and scent.*
> *To come out is to be caught; I cannot hide from You.*[14]

Marie Howe's work describes how the ordinary is shot through with the transcendent in every moment, if we could but see it that way. She is one of the few unabashedly religious poets writing today, and yet her subject is always the mundanity of daily living, not some exalted religious experience or deferral to dogma or received belief. Her poem "What the Living Do" addresses her dead brother with these lines:

> *But there are moments, walking, when I catch a glimpse of*
> *myself in the window glass,*
> *say, the window of the corner video store, and I'm gripped*
> *by a cherishing so deep*
>
> *for my own blowing hair, chapped face, and unbuttoned*
> *coat that I'm speechless:*
> *I am living, I remember you.*

It is no accident that "Annunciation" appears in her book *The Kingdom of Ordinary Time.* Marie Howe grew up in an Irish Catholic family and was deeply affected by Catholic ritual from an early age. She sang Bach masses in the choir of her school, the Academy of the Sacred Heart, and would be moved to tears by the beauty of the experience. This was pure prayer for her, singing, as she has said, "to the higher power, the great spirit, all that is."

The phrase *ordinary time* points to her intent in the book but also to her interest in general — the conjunction of the sacred and the secular. In the Roman Catholic liturgical calendar, the term *ordinary time* refers to Sundays that are not holy feast days. The ecclesiastical "ordinary" is the part of the Mass that does not change from day to day. So Howe is weaving together these definitions with the literal meaning of *ordinary*, what Mary Oliver in her poem "Mindful" calls

> *the common, the very drab,*
> *the daily presentations.*

"Annunciation" looks at Mary's life from a contemporary perspective. Howe imagines in this poem the moment after Mary has experienced the annunciation and is reflecting on what just happened. Again, there is no mention of Christ or an angel, no biblical reference of any kind. Howe's Mary is a woman like any woman, her mind engaged in an internal dialogue, in awe of the mystery.

In an interview with Kim Rosen for *Spirituality & Health* magazine, Howe said:

> Those poems in the voice of Mary really were another voice speaking. I showed four of them to [my mentor] Stanley Kunitz and he said, "Now you must write an Annunciation poem." I said, "I can't do that! I can write about her bewilderment. I can write about her tentative sightings of something. I can't write about Annunciation."
>
> But I tried. I wrote a whole bunch of them and just threw them out. Then, as usual, when I finally

gave up, this voice came: "Even if I don't see it again
— nor ever feel it / I know it is."[...]

The greatest joy for me is when my will is finally
exhausted. Then something else can speak.

"Something else can speak": this is itself an annunciation,
and it usually happens for writers when we have given up in
the face of the blank page. Artists of all kinds know this; we
all know it in our own way. In her own Annunciation poem,
Denise Levertov wrote:

> *aren't there annunciations*
> *of one sort or another in most lives?*

Indeed there are. We can be blessed at any moment by the
startling realization that who we are is so much vaster than
our familiar identity, with its furniture of well-worn thoughts
and feelings, hopes, and fears; that something else in us can
speak with a voice that knows what the mind does not know:
that we are loved, no matter what.

Just linger for a moment, now that we have come to the
end of this book, and savor your own experience of these ex-
traordinary lines, at once so mysterious and yet somehow so
achingly recognizable:

> *and so it is myself I want to turn in that direction*
> *not as toward a place, but it was a tilting*
> *within myself,*

as one turns a mirror to flash the light to where
it isn't — I was blinded like that — and swam
in what shone at me

only able to endure it by being no one and so
specifically myself I thought I'd die
from being loved like that.

Howe feels a "tilting" within herself, a reorientation, as it were; a recalibration that turns her inner gaze, her awareness, back on itself and blinds her with its light. Her familiar self has to be blinded — she has to become no one — in order to experience her true personhood, her unique core in which she knows absolutely that she is always and forever loved. May we, each in our own way, feel that tilting within ourselves, and know, whatever outer difficulties we may be facing in our life,

that if once it hailed me
it ever does.

PERMISSIONS ACKNOWLEDGMENTS

NOTES

1. Sylvia Plath, "Fever 103°," in *The Collected Poems of Sylvia Plath*, ed. Ted Hughes (New York: HarperCollins, 1966 and 1994).

2. Jane Hirshfield, private conversation with the author.

3. John Keats in a letter to John Taylor, February 1818, in *Keats: Poems and Selected Letters*, ed. Carlos Baker (New York: Scribner, 1962).

4. Saul Bellow, quoted in Azar Nafisi, *Reading Lolita in Tehran: A Memoir in Books* (New York: Random House, 2003).

5. Conrad Aiken, *Ushant* (New York: Oxford University Press, 1971).

6. W. B. Yeats, *The Collected Works of William Butler Yeats*, ed. Allan Wade (London: Chapman & Hall, 1908), introduction.

7. James Dickey, *Babel to Byzantium: Poets and Poetry Now* (New York: Farrar Straus & Giroux, 1981).

8. Kim Stafford, *Early Morning: Remembering My Father, William Stafford* (Minneapolis: Graywolf Press, 2002).

9. William Stafford, *The Answers Are Inside the Mountains: Meditations on the Writing Life* (Ann Arbor, MI: University of Michigan Press, 2003).

10. Roger Housden, *For Lovers of God Everywhere: Poems of the Christian Mystics* (Carlsbad, CA: Hay House, 2009).

11. Breen Jenkins, private conversation with the author.

12. Wendell Berry, "Why," in *Given: Poems* (Berkeley, CA: Counterpoint, 2006).

13. Nazim Hikmet, "In the Snowy Night Woods," in *Poems of Nazim Hikmet*, trans. Randy Blasing and Mutlu Konuk (New York: Norton, 2002).

14. Jacopone da Todi, "How the Soul through the Senses Finds God in All Creatures," in Housden, *For Lovers of God*.

ABOUT THE POETS

CONRAD AIKEN (1889–1973)
Conrad Aiken was born in Savannah, Georgia. After the death of his parents, he was brought up by a great-great-aunt in Massachusetts and then attended Harvard in 1912. His first collection of poetry, *Earth Triumphant*, was published in 1914 and quickly established his reputation as a poet. Much of his work reflects a deep interest in psychoanalysis and the development of identity. Aiken published thirty-three volumes of poetry, including his *Collected Poems*, which won the National Book Award in 1924.

ELLEN BASS (B. 1947)
Billy Collins said of Ellen Bass's work that her "frighteningly personal poems about sex, love, birth, motherhood, and aging are kept from mere confession by the graces of wit, an observant eye, an empathetic heart, and just the right image deployed at just the right time." Bass is the author of several nonfiction books, including *The Courage to Heal*, which has been translated into nine languages. Her poetry collection

Mules of Love won the Lambda Literary Award, and she has also won the Pushcart Prize and the Pablo Neruda Prize for poetry. Her most recent collection is *Like a Beggar*.

WENDELL BERRY (B. 1934)

Wendell Berry, a farmer with an intense interest in our relationship to the land and in sustainable living, lives in his native Kentucky. He is the author of more than thirty books of poetry, essays, and novels. A reviewer for the *Christian Science Monitor* writes that "Berry's poems shine with the gentle wisdom of a craftsman who has thought deeply about the paradoxical strangeness and wonder of life."

JACK GILBERT (1925–2012)

Jack Gilbert, born in Pittsburgh, was educated both in his hometown and in San Francisco. Soon after publishing his first book of poems, in 1962, he went on a Guggenheim Fellowship to Europe, where he stayed for many years, mostly in Greece. *Monolithos*, his second volume, was published twenty years after his first. Gilbert always avoided the beaten track to success and recognition, preferring the authenticity of a life on a remote Greek island to the ambitions of New York City. The poet James Dickey once said, "He takes himself away to a place more inward than it is safe to go; from that awful silence and tightening, he returns to us poems of savage compassion." Gilbert's *Refusing Heaven*, published in 2005, won the National Book Critics Circle Award.

Nazim Hikmet (1902–1963)

Raised in Istanbul, Nazim left Allied-occupied Turkey after the First World War and ended up in Moscow, where he attended university and met writers and artists from all over the world. After Turkish Independence in 1924 he returned to Turkey but was soon arrested for working on a leftist magazine. He managed to escape to Russia, where he continued to write plays and poems. In 1928 a general amnesty allowed Nazim to return to Turkey, and during the next ten years he published nine books of poetry — five collections and four long poems — while working as a proofreader, journalist, scriptwriter, and translator. He left Turkey for the last time in 1951, after serving a lengthy jail sentence for his radical acts, and lived in the Soviet Union and Eastern Europe, where he continued to work for the ideals of world Communism. Nazim died of a heart attack in Moscow in 1963. The first modern Turkish poet, he is recognized around the world as one of the great international poets of the twentieth century.

Marie Howe (b. 1950)

The poet Stanley Kunitz says, "Howe's long, deep-breathing lines address the mysteries of flesh and spirit, in terms accessible only to a woman who is very much of our time and yet still in touch with the sacred." Howe's poems have appeared in *The New Yorker*, the *Atlantic Monthly*, and the *Harvard Review*, among other publications. She is the author of a number of poetry collections, including, in 2017, *Magdalene: Poems*. Hers is a poetry of intimacy, witness, honesty, and relation.

W. S. MERWIN (B. 1927)

W. S. Merwin was born in New York, the son of a Presbyterian minister; the earliest influence on his life as a poet was his love of hymns. On graduating from Princeton, he lived and traveled in Europe, working as a scriptwriter, playwright, and teacher. He now lives in Maui, where he and his late wife made their home on a pineapple plantation, which they transformed into a palm tree preserve. A main concern and theme in his work is the separation of humans from nature and their destruction of the environment. His most recent collections are *The Shadow of Sirius* (2009), for which Merwin won his second Pulitzer Prize; *The Moon before Morning* (2015); and *Garden Time* (2016).

JAN RICHARDSON (B. 1967)

Jan Richardson is the director of the Wellspring Studio, publishing works that blend her art and writing, and she offers her services as a retreat and conference speaker. After serving at a United Methodist Church in Orlando, Richardson developed a full-time ministry in the arts. She served as artist in residence at a retreat center owned by the Catholic Diocese of Orlando, and for eleven years offered a creative worship service at First United Methodist Church in Winter Park, Florida. Her creative work is her ministry: she paints, draws and makes collages, and writes poetry and essays. Her husband, Garrison Doles, was her partner in ministry until his unexpected death of a brain aneurysm in 2013. Richardson's experience of grieving has been an intrinsic part of her spiritual journey since then and is reflected in many of her poems and paintings. *Circle of Grace: A Book of Blessings for the Seasons*, was published in 2015. *The Cure for Sorrow*, a poetry collection, was published in 2016.

MAGGIE SMITH (B. 1977)

Maggie Smith is the author of three poetry collections: *Good Bones* (2017), *The Well Speaks of Its Own Poison* (2015), and *Lamp of the Body* (2005). Smith is also the author of three prize-winning chapbooks. She has taught creative writing at Gettysburg College (2003–2004) and in the MFA program at Ohio State University (2016), and she worked for several years in trade book and educational publishing. Smith now lives with her husband and two children in Bexley, Ohio, where she works as a freelance writer and editor, and serves as a consulting editor to *The Kenyon Review*.

WILLIAM STAFFORD (1914–1993)

Stafford was born in Hutchinson, Kansas, the oldest of three children in a highly literate family. During the Depression his family moved from town to town in an effort to find work for his father. A pacifist and one of "the quiet of the land," as he often describes himself, Stafford was known for his unique method of composition, his soft voice, and his independence from social and literary expectations. Stafford was forty-six years old when his first major poetry collection,

Traveling through the Dark, which won the 1963 National Book Award for Poetry, was published. Stafford was a close friend of and collaborator with poet Robert Bly. Despite his late start, he was a frequent contributor to magazines and anthologies and eventually published fifty-seven volumes of poetry.

ABOUT THE AUTHOR

Roger Housden is the author of twenty-three books, including the bestselling Ten Poems series. All his books explore perennial human questions through the use of poetry, art, or pilgrimage. His work has been featured in the *New York Times*, the *Los Angeles Times*, and *O, The Oprah Magazine*. Housden uses writing as a teaching tool for personal exploration and reflection and teaches courses around the country.

www.rogerhousden.com

NEW WORLD LIBRARY is dedicated to publishing books and other media that inspire and challenge us to improve the quality of our lives and the world.

We are a socially and environmentally aware company. We recognize that we have an ethical responsibility to our customers, our staff members, and our planet.

We serve our customers by creating the finest publications possible on personal growth, creativity, spirituality, wellness, and other areas of emerging importance. We serve New World Library employees with generous benefits, significant profit sharing, and constant encouragement to pursue their most expansive dreams.

As a member of the Green Press Initiative, we print an increasing number of books with soy-based ink on 100 percent postconsumer-waste recycled paper. Also, we power our offices with solar energy and contribute to non-profit organizations working to make the world a better place for us all.

Our products are available in bookstores everywhere.

www.newworldlibrary.com

At NewWorldLibrary.com you can download our catalog,
subscribe to our e-newsletter, read our blog,
and link to authors' websites, videos, and podcasts.

Find us on Facebook, follow us on Twitter, and watch us on YouTube.

Send your questions and comments our way!
You make it possible for us to do what we love to do.

Phone: 415-884-2100 or 800-972-6657
Catalog requests: Ext. 10 | Orders: Ext. 10 | Fax: 415-884-2199
escort@newworldlibrary.com

NEW WORLD LIBRARY
publishing books that change lives   14 Pamaron Way, Novato, CA 94949